T0146972

An Analysis of

Ian Kershaw's

The "Hitler Myth": Image and Reality in the Third Reich

Helen Roche

Published by Macat International Ltd
24:13 Coda Centre, 189 Munster Road, London SW6 6AW.

Distributed exclusively by Routledge
2 Park Square, Milton Park, Abingdon, Oxon OX14 4RN
711 Third Avenue, New York, NY 10017, USA

Routledge is an imprint of the Taylor & Francis Group, an informa business

www.macat.com
info@macat.com

Cataloguing in Publication Data
A catalogue record for this book is available from the British Library.
Library of Congress Cataloguing-in-Publication Data is available upon request.
Cover illustration: Etienne Gilfillan

ISBN 978-1-912302-69-7 (hardback)
ISBN 978-1-912128-56-3 (paperback)
ISBN 978-1-912281-57-2 (e-book)

Notice
The information in this book is designed to orientate readers of the work under analysis,
to elucidate and contextualise its key ideas and themes, and to aid in the development
of critical thinking skills. It is not meant to be used, nor should it be used, as a
substitute for original thinking or in place of original writing or research. References and
notes are provided for informational purposes and their presence does not constitute
endorsement of the information or opinions therein. This book is presented solely for
educational purposes. It is sold on the understanding that the publisher is not engaged
to provide any scholarly advice. The publisher has made every effort to ensure that
this book is accurate and up-to-date, but makes no warranties or representations with
regard to the completeness or reliability of the information it contains. The information
and the opinions provided herein are not guaranteed or warranted to produce particular
results and may not be suitable for students of every ability. The publisher shall not be
liable for any loss, damage or disruption arising from any errors or omissions, or from
the use of this book, including, but not limited to, special, incidental, consequential or
other damages caused, or alleged to have been caused, directly or indirectly, by the
information contained within.

'Macat is taking on some of the major challenges in university education ... They have drawn together a strong team of active academics who are producing teaching materials that are novel in the breadth of their approach.'

Prof Lord Broers,
former Vice-Chancellor of the University of Cambridge

'The Macat vision is exceptionally exciting. It focuses upon new modes of learning which analyse and explain seminal texts which have profoundly influenced world thinking and so social and economic development. It promotes the kind of critical thinking which is essential for any society and economy.
This is the learning of the future.'

Rt Hon Charles Clarke, former UK Secretary of State for Education

'The Macat analyses provide immediate access to the critical conversation surrounding the books that have shaped their respective discipline, which will make them an invaluable resource to all of those, students and teachers, working in the field.'

Professor William Tronzo, University of California at San Diego

'Listening to classical music or jazz without having had a musical training, you can like the piece, but you don't know why or even what the musician/composer is doing in it, let alone its significance in the history of music as a whole. Similarly there is so much implicit in an academic text that to read it out of the context in which it is written requires some pointers to help you understand the author, their concerns, and what they were responding to; in short, the intellectual history of the work. This is where Macat comes in, not as a substitute but as an essential complement to the writing of seminal figures in the history of a discipline.'

Tristam Barrett, University of Cambridge

ABOUT THE AUTHOR OF THE ORIGINAL WORK
Sir Ian Kershaw is a British historian, and one of the world's greatest living experts on Nazi Germany. Born in Oldham in 1943, Kershaw began his academic career as a scholar of medieval history, but soon found himself drawn to the modern era. After taking up a post in Germany in 1975, his growing interest in the Nazi regime led him to publish *The 'Hitler Myth': Image and Reality in the Third Reich* in 1980. He went on to base himself at the University of Sheffield and to write a series of best-selling works on the same period, including a two-volume biography of Hitler that has since become the standard work on the subject. Kershaw was knighted for his services to history in 2002.

ABOUT THE AUTHOR OF THE ANALYSIS
Dr Helen Roche teaches history at the University of Cambridge, where her work focuses on education and the uses of classicism in Nazi Germany. She is the author of *Sparta's German Children: The Ideal of Ancient Sparta in the Royal Prussian Cadet Corps, 1818-1920, and in National-Socialist elite schools (the Napolas),* and her second monograph, *The Third Reich's Elite Schools: A History of the Napolas,* is forthcoming from Oxford University Press.

ABOUT THIS BOOK

This book is part of a series of unique academic explorations of seminal works in the humanities and social sciences – books and papers that have had a significant and widely recognised impact on their disciplines. It has been created to serve as much more than just a summary of what lies between the covers of a great book. It illuminates and explores the influences on, ideas of, and impact of that book. Our goal is to offer a learning resource that encourages critical thinking and fosters a better, deeper understanding of important ideas.

Each publication is divided into three parts, which we call Sections. They are: Influences, Ideas, and Impact.

Each Section has four chapters, which we call Modules. These explore every important facet of the work, and the responses to it. You can find a list in the Contents.

This Section-Module structure makes a Macat book easy to use, but it has another important feature. Because each Macat book is written to the same format, it is possible (and encouraged!) to cross-reference multiple Macat books along the same lines of inquiry or research. This allows the reader to open up interesting interdisciplinary pathways.

To further aid your reading, lists of glossary terms and people mentioned are included at the end of this book (these are indicated by an asterisk [*] throughout) – as well as a list of works cited.

We've partnered with some of the best academic minds in the world to produce these publications.

We hope you enjoy your Macat journey. Read this book critically and let us know what you think at **www.macat.com.**

CRITICAL THINKING AND *THE 'HITLER MYTH'*

Primary critical thinking skill: PROBLEM-SOLVING
Secondary critical thinking skill: EVALUATION

Few historical problems are more baffling in retrospect than the conundrum of how Hitler was able to rise to power in Germany and then command the German people – many of whom had only marginal interest in or affiliation to Nazism – and the Nazi state. It took Ian Kershaw – author of the standard two-volume biography of Hitler – to provide a truly convincing solution to this problem. Kershaw's model blends theory – notably Max Weber's concept of 'charismatic leadership' – with new archival research into the development of the Hitler 'cult' from its origins in the 1920s to its collapse in the face of the harsh realities of the latter stages of World War II. Kershaw's model also looks at dictatorship from an unusual angle: not from the top down, but from the bottom up, seeking to understand what ordinary Germans thought about their leader.

Kershaw's broad approach is a problem-solving one. Most obviously, he actively interrogates his evidence, asking highly productive questions that lead him to fresh understandings and help generate solutions that are credibly rooted in the archives. Kershaw's theories also have application elsewhere; the model set out in The 'Hitler Myth' has been used to analyse other charismatic leaders, including several from ideologically-opposed backgrounds.

Macat has worked with the University of Cambridge to identify the elements of critical thinking and understand the ways in which six different skills combine to enable effective thinking. Three allow us to fully understand a problem; three more give us the tools to solve it. Together, these six skills make up the **PACIER** model of critical thinking. They are:

ANALYSIS – understanding how an argument is built
EVALUATION – exploring the strengths and weaknesses of an argument
INTERPRETATION – understanding issues of meaning

CREATIVE THINKING – coming up with new ideas and fresh connections
PROBLEM-SOLVING – producing strong solutions
REASONING – creating strong arguments

To find out more, visit **WWW.MACAT.COM.**

CONTENTS

WAYS IN TO THE TEXT

KEY POINTS

- Born in 1943, the British historian Ian Kershaw is one of the world's greatest living experts on Germany under the regime of the Nazis* (the far-right National Socialist Party, led by Adolf Hitler* from 1921 until the defeat of Nazi Germany in 1945).

- First published in Germany in 1980, *The "Hitler Myth"* tries to explain Hitler's widespread popularity among the German people, even as he led them into global conflict and genocide* (the mass killing of a group of people, particularly on ethnic grounds).

- Kershaw's use of the term "myth" to define a political leader's personality cult has been widely used in history and other disciplines.

Who Is Ian Kershaw?

Ian Kershaw was born in 1943 in the town of Oldham, near Manchester, England. His mother worked in a cotton mill, and his father played the saxophone and clarinet in dance bands. Though his family was never well off, Kershaw still managed to get an excellent education by winning a place at the respected St Bede's College in Manchester. He went on to study medieval history at university, first at Liverpool, then as a doctoral student at Oxford. He then took up a lectureship in medieval history at Manchester University.[1]

While preparing to work on European peasant revolts, however, Kershaw began learning German. As he did so, he became more and more interested in contemporary German history and politics. He then started researching social history in Nazi Germany. Coincidentally, a lectureship in modern history had just been advertised at Manchester; Kershaw applied, and got the job. Soon afterward, in 1975, he was offered a post by the director of the *Institut für Zeitgeschichte* (Institute for Contemporary History)* in Munich (at that time, prior to the 1990 German reunification, located in West Germany). The position was part of a large-scale research project on Nazism in the German region of Bavaria.*[2]

Using research from his time in Munich, Kershaw published two books, including *The "Hitler Myth": Image and Reality in the Third Reich*. He then went on to write many other best-selling works on Nazi Germany, including a classic two-volume biography of Adolf Hitler. He was professor of Modern History at Nottingham University in England from 1987 to 1989, and then at Sheffield University, also in the UK, from 1989 to 2008. In 2002 he was knighted for services to history.[3]

What Does *The "Hitler Myth"* Say?

Following new trends in German history after World War II,* Ian Kershaw wanted to focus on the "history of everyday life." So *The "Hitler Myth"* concentrated on the general public's attitudes to Hitler, rather than taking a "top-down" approach looking at the actions and motives of people of high status. Kershaw was looking for an answer to the question "How could Hitler happen?" Why did so many Germans allow the brutality and criminality of Nazi rule?

In trying to explain the popularity that Hitler enjoyed among the German people, Kershaw looked at the way in which Hitler's image was constructed through propaganda*—politically influential messages disseminated through the media. Using fresh sources from the archives, he explored ordinary Germans' own views of the dictator* (a national leader whose power is absolute). He charted the growth of the cult of Hitler during the 1920s and early 1930s, culminating in Germany's victory over France in 1940.

One reason for Hitler's enduring popularity, Kershaw believed, could be found in the charismatic nature of his leadership. In making his case, Kershaw drew on ideas relating to political power and charismatic leadership* put forward by Max Weber,* whose inquiry into social structures and behavior made him a pioneer in the field of sociology.* The German people, Kershaw argued, were fixated on Hitler as a heroic savior figure, deserving of the greatest personal loyalty and trust. They mostly saw the regime's failures as the fault of Hitler's corrupt underlings, never as the result of his own decisions; triumphs in foreign policy or economic upturns, meanwhile, were credited to Hitler's unique talents and achievements. The power of the "Hitler myth" started to wane only when it became obvious that World War II could only end in defeat. Even then, many Germans believed their leader might still save them right until the very end.

The "Hitler Myth" is a vital resource for anyone working on the political or social history of the Third Reich* (the term used for Germany between 1933 and 1945, when it was ruled by Hitler and the National Socialist [Nazi] regime). Since its first edition appeared in German in 1980, *The "Hitler Myth"* has been published in multiple editions and translated into many languages.[4] Most importantly, it has popularized the concept of the "Hitler myth." This has not only given rise to spin-off works considering other aspects of this "myth," but it has also proved a useful tool for analyzing other movements or regimes with similar leadership cults, such as that of the Soviet Union.*[5]

Moreover, by showing how Hitler came to have such a hold over ordinary Germans, the book helps to explain their acceptance of Nazi crimes. World War II was one of the most destructive wars ever fought, and the Holocaust*—the mass murder of approximately six million

Jews* and other minorities by the Nazi regime between 1941 and 1945—was one of the largest mass killings in human history. Hitler and his followers were responsible for both. If we can understand how Hitler came to lead the German people "into the abyss," then we gain an understanding of how such slaughter became possible.[6] We might even be better able to guard against similar atrocities happening in the future.

Why Does *The "Hitler Myth"* Matter?

The "Hitler Myth" is not only an important book for people studying the Third Reich, or even for historians generally—scholars in many other disciplines have also found its ideas and concepts useful. For instance, Kershaw's use of the term "myth" to describe the propaganda cult around Hitler has been taken up by sociologists and political scientists. Kershaw's ideas about Hitler's "charismatic leadership" have also resonated far beyond historians of Nazi Germany. More recently, the idea has been used to analyze leaders of present-day right-wing movements. Even if the idea is not always seen as applying directly to the leaders in question, scholars still find it a useful tool.[7]

The "Hitler Myth" can also point toward wider political trends. Leadership cults developed in many other countries across the world during the twentieth century. This form of propaganda swiftly became a global phenomenon, under fascist* and communist* regimes alike. Students of transnationalism* (an approach to history that tries to make connections between different countries, rather than focusing on individual nation-states) or global change can find useful points of comparison. Indeed, when we look at modern dictatorships, some of Kershaw's ideas may still be helpful.

Part of the value of *The "Hitler Myth"* is that it does not deal purely with historical events. Nor is it an example of traditional "great man" history (an approach to historical analysis centered on the ideas and achievements of specific figures considered to be particularly significant). More interestingly, the book explores the dynamics of power between rulers and those who are ruled. It looks at dictatorship from the bottom up, through the eyes of ordinary people. In so doing, it provides one answer to the problem of how an individual can climb to become an important political figure and establish authority as a dictator. It also illustrates the dangers of becoming enchanted by any personality cult. This is particularly dangerous in an age where the media can make this process all the more powerful. Hitler was perhaps the best example of a politician who used new media, such as radio, to reinforce the myth-making process. *The "Hitler Myth"* could be said to demonstrate the need for some measure of skepticism and doubt in our own lives. Sometimes, it may be tempting to trust in the promise of political salvation a powerful leader might offer. In practice, though, that "salvation" is rarely worth the price.

NOTES

1   Stephen Moss, "A Life in Writing: Ian Kershaw," *Guardian*, August 17, 2011; Danny Millum, interview with Ian Kershaw, May 14, 2008, accessed October 2015, http://www.history.ac.uk/makinghistory/resources/interviews/Kershaw_Ian.html.

2   Millum, "Interview"; Moss, "A Life in Writing."

3   Sheffield University Library, "The Sir Ian Kershaw Collection," accessed November 2015, http://www.sheffield.ac.uk/library/special/kershaw.

4   Ian Kershaw, *The "Hitler Myth": Image and Reality in the Third Reich* (Oxford: Oxford University Press, 2001), ix.

5   See, for example, Ian Kershaw and Moshe Lewin, eds., *Stalinism and Nazism: Dictatorships in Comparison* (Cambridge: Cambridge University Press, 1997); Michael Geyer and Sheila Fitzpatrick, eds., *Beyond Totalitarianism: Stalinism and Nazism Compared* (Cambridge: Cambridge University Press, 2009).

6   See Laurence Rees, *The Dark Charisma of Adolf Hitler: Leading Millions into the Abyss* (London: Ebury Press, 2013).

7   See, for example, Roger Eatwell, "The Rebirth of Right-Wing Charisma? The Cases of Jean-Marie le Pen and Vladimir Zhirinovsky," Totalitarian *Movements and Political Religions* 3, no. 3 (2002): 1–23.

SECTION 1
INFLUENCES

THE AUTHOR AND THE HISTORICAL CONTEXT

KEY POINTS

- The "*Hitler Myth*" is still one of the most important works considering the impact on ordinary Germans of Adolf Hitler's* image, fueled by propaganda.*

- Kershaw was first inspired to research modern German history while taking language courses in Manchester and Munich.

- In so doing, Kershaw made a radical career change from researching medieval history, his previous specialism.

Why Read this Text?

Ian Kershaw's *The "Hitler Myth": Image and Reality in the Third Reich*, first published in 1980, is still one of the most important and widely cited works on Hitler's relationship with the German people. It provides a convincing chronological account of the development of Adolf Hitler's charismatic hold over ordinary Germans. From uncertain beginnings in the Weimar Republic* (as Germany was known between 1919, after World War I,* and 1933), Hitler's popularity reached its peak after his heady foreign-policy successes of the late 1930s and his lightning victories early in World War II.* Thereafter, people slowly began to lose faith in him, as Germany's defeat at the hands of the Allies*—the coalition led by Great Britain, the Soviet Union,* and the United States—came to seem more and more inevitable.

As well as highlighting the importance of public opinion and popular consent in supporting the Nazi* regime, *The "Hitler Myth"*

> ❝ I think it has helped that I've never had any personal connection to the Nazi period, as none of my family died in the war. I was once asked in Germany if I could really be sure that none of my relatives had committed atrocities. I said I could be reasonably confident my Dad hadn't. He spent the war running the dance band at RAF* Abingdon. ❞
>
> Ian Kershaw, "Ian Kershaw: Post Master," *Guardian*

also put forward some useful theoretical concepts. Foremost among these was the idea that Hitler's hold on his people could best be illuminated by the theory of "charismatic leadership"* proposed by the pioneering sociologist* Max Weber.*

In his famous essay "Politics as a Vocation" (first delivered as a lecture in 1919), Weber had developed the idea of a certain sort of political authority, "charismatic authority," which depended entirely upon "a certain quality of an individual personality, by virtue of which he is set apart from ordinary men and treated as endowed with supernatural, superhuman, or at least specifically exceptional powers or qualities." Weber distinguished this type of authority from more bureaucratic "traditional" or "legal" forms of leadership. He also highlighted that the most important aspect of a charismatic leader's power was how he was "actually regarded by… his 'followers' or 'disciples.'"[1]

Although Kershaw was not the first to suggest a connection between Weber's theory and Hitler's* rule, it was Kershaw's in-depth use of the concept that popularized the idea more widely.[2] Rather than merely likening Hitler superficially to the charismatic leaders in primitive societies that Weber had discussed, Kershaw extended his framework of interpretation in order to illuminate Hitler's broader relationship with the German people.[3]

Finally, the term "myth" as used by Kershaw to describe Hitler's image that was fueled by propaganda (that is, misleading information circulated with the aim of influencing an audience to adopt a particular— commonly political— opinion) has since been applied to many other dictatorships and extremist movements, as well as having become a term of art* in studies of the Third Reich*—the Nazi regime.[4]

Author's Life

Ian Kershaw was born in the town of Oldham, near Manchester, England, in 1943. Despite his family's relative poverty, Kershaw was able to gain a good education by winning a place at St Bede's College, a Roman Catholic* grammar school in Manchester, where his history teacher instilled in him a deep love of the subject. He then went on to read medieval history at Liverpool University, before completing a doctorate at Merton College, Oxford, on the accounts of a medieval monastery called Bolton Priory.*[5]

While studying German at the Goethe Institute* in preparation for a project on the history of medieval peasant revolts in Europe, Kershaw became increasingly drawn to the more recent German past. He successfully applied for a job in the modern history department at Manchester University, where he had previously held a lectureship in medieval history. He began to research popular opinion in Nazi Germany, and was very soon invited to join a large-scale project, "Bavaria* in the National Socialist era," run by the German historian Martin Broszat,* director of the *Institut für Zeitgeschichte* (Institute for Contemporary History)* in Munich, the capital of Bavaria.[6]

Working on the "Bavaria project" was, for Kershaw, to be the start of a long-standing engagement with the history of the Third Reich that has lasted to this day. Following his two books based on the project, *The "Hitler Myth"* and *Popular Opinion and Political Dissent in the Third Reich*, Kershaw went on to write a series of best-selling works on Hitler's life, including a two-volume biography that has since become the standard work on the subject. He is now considered one of the world's greatest living experts on Nazi Germany, and in 2002 he was knighted for his services to history.[7]

Author's Background

Kershaw believes that his somewhat unorthodox career path—switching from medieval to modern history—was only possible because of the less-regulated nature of university life in the 1970s and 1980s, saying, "I don't think you'd be able to do it now with [the current system of government assessment for research grants]—it was difficult enough then."[8]

His decision to make this change was substantially conditioned by the political situation at the time that he first started taking an interest in German culture. In an interview in 2007 with the British newspaper *the Guardian*, referencing the radical political activity that swept Europe in 1968, he noted the sudden nature of his choice: "As my German improved I became very interested in what was happening in Germany—it was just after the 1968 student revolutions,* there was a lot happening and the Nazi period wasn't that far away—and how [Germany] was coping with the legacy of the war."[9]

His resolve to forget medieval peasants and concentrate on contemporary history was also hardened by an encounter in 1972 with a former Nazi in Munich, where he was taking a language course: "I met this fellow, and he asked me what I was doing there. He said: 'You English, you were so stupid, you should have been in the war with us. We'd have defeated the Bolsheviks* and divided the world up between us.' And he said at one point: 'The Jew* is a louse.' I was completely shocked by this, and it made me wonder what went on in this little place at that time. That was the trigger, but I was already on the way."[10]

NOTES

1 Max Weber, "Politics as a Vocation" (1919), quoted in Ian Kershaw, *The "Hitler Myth": Image and Reality in the Third Reich* (Oxford: Oxford University Press, 2001), 8.

2 See Michel Dobry, "Hitler, Charisma and Structure: Reflections on Historical Methodology," in *Charisma and Fascism in Interwar Europe*, eds. António Costa Pinto, Roger Eatwell, and Stein Igelvik Larsen (New York: Routledge, 2007), 20.

3 Kershaw, *"Hitler Myth"*, 9.

4 See, for example, Ian Kershaw and Moshe Lewin, eds., *Stalinism and Nazism: Dictatorships in Comparison* (Cambridge: Cambridge University Press, 1997); Roger Eatwell, "The Rebirth of Right-Wing Charisma? The Cases of Jean-Marie le Pen and Vladimir Zhirinovsky," *Totalitarian Movements and Political Religions* 3, no. 3 (2002): 1–23.

5 Stephen Moss, "A Life in Writing: Ian Kershaw," *Guardian*, August 17, 2011.

6 Danny Millum, interview with Ian Kershaw, May 14, 2008, accessed October 2015, *http://www.history.ac.uk/makinghistory/resources/interviews/Kershaw_Ian.html.*

7 Sheffield University Library, "The Sir Ian Kershaw Collection," accessed November 2015, http://www.sheffield.ac.uk/library/special/kershaw.

8 Millum, "Interview."

9 Moss, "A Life in Writing."

10 Moss, "A Life in Writing."

ACADEMIC CONTEXT

KEY POINTS

- *The "Hitler Myth"* reflects German historians' broader preoccupation with the Nazi* past in the decades following World War II.*

- The book is deeply rooted in the German tradition of researching the history of everyday life *(Alltagsgeschichte)** that came to the fore in the later 1970s and 1980s.

- While writing *The "Hitler Myth"*, Kershaw was influenced most fundamentally by his collaboration with colleagues at the Institute for Contemporary History (*Institut für Zeitgeschichte)** in Munich.

The Work In Its Context

Following World War II, Germany was divided into two—a division that still existed when Ian Kershaw wrote *The "Hitler Myth": Image and Reality in the Third Reich*. The so-called Iron Curtain* marked the boundary between the communist* German Democratic Republic* to the east and the democratic Federal Republic of Germany* to the west; on each side, history—notably the toxic legacy of Nazism—was crucial in shaping the direction in which historians took their research.[1]

From the late 1940s onwards, the Allies,* and in particular the Americans, had been keen to sponsor historical investigations into the Nazi past, and had collaborated with the West German and Bavarian* governments to found a research center that would focus on this type of "contemporary history." This initiative resulted in the birth of the *Institut für Zeitgeschichte* (Institute for Contemporary History) in Munich in 1950.[2]

> **❝** The overriding concern of research in Germany on how the Nazi system had been possible, then into how it functioned … was crucial. The early consciously self-critical 'contemporary history' saw itself as engaged in vital work of clarification for a new, uncertain democracy still feeling its way. **❞**
>
> Ian Kershaw, "Beware the Moral High Ground," *Times Literary Supplement*

It was there, in the 1970s, that Ian Kershaw began the research that would ultimately result in the publication of *The "Hitler Myth"*. Scholars at the *Institut* were then keen to move beyond the prevailing fashion for institutional "top-down" histories of the Third Reich* that focused on the actions of those of political and military influence and importance. They wanted, rather, to discover how the man on the street had been affected by the Nazi regime.[3] In seeking to answer one of contemporary historians' burning questions—"How did Hitler* happen?"—by investigating Adolf Hitler's reputation among ordinary Germans, Kershaw's inquiry therefore fitted perfectly into the current research interests of the *Institut*.[4]

Overview of the Field

One of the hallmarks of this new movement in German historical studies was the shift toward what is now known as *Alltagsgeschichte*—the history of everyday life. This was a specifically German variant of the burgeoning interest in social history*—that is, historical inquiry focusing on the experiences of ordinary people rather than the actions of "great men"— that could be seen in universities throughout the Western world at this time. Its roots lay in the dissatisfaction that the younger generation of German historians felt with the forms of "structural history" (*Strukturgeschichte*)* advocated by the so-called Bielefeld School.* This latter group of scholars, foremost among them Hans-Ulrich Wehler* and Jürgen Kocka,* tended to focus on "an abstract analysis of the large structures and long-term historical processes that created a German *Sonderweg* (special path) leading to Hitler." By contrast, *Alltagsgeschichte* sought to uncover the culture and experiences of ordinary people and the working classes.[5]

At this time, the German historical establishment was also utterly polarized over the question of whether Hitler had been the prime mover behind the Third Reich's murderous policies, or whether he had merely been a "weak dictator,"* caught up in bureaucratic structures that had pushed these policies forward with a momentum all their own. In this debate between the "intentionalists"* (who saw Hitler's own intentions and ideological motivations as key) and the "functionalists"* or "structuralists" (according to whom responsibility ultimately lay with structural elements within the state such as the Nazi Party and the SS, the elite corps responsible for the police and terror apparatus), Kershaw tended to stand in the latter camp.[6] However, his work on Hitler's public image in Bavaria can be seen as a way of exploring the dictator's power that also took account of the prevailing trend toward exploring regional micro-histories,* rather than merely focusing upon the actions of elites, institutions, and bureaucracies[7] ("micro-history" refers to the analysis of a specific event, individual, or community rather than a larger historical current or period).

Academic Influences

Given Kershaw's abrupt shift from researching medieval British history to studying modern German history, many of his earliest mentors and influences, such as Christopher Brooke* and Eric Stone,* had little impact on his subsequent development as a historian of the Third Reich. However, Kershaw does name a number of British historians of Germany, including Timothy Mason,* William Carr,* and Alan Milward,* as being "tremendously important to me as a novice in the field."[8]

That said, he names his most important intellectual influences as his senior colleagues at the Institute for Contemporary History in Munich, with whom he worked from the 1970s onwards. He describes Martin

Broszat* (then director of the Institute, and principal investigator of "Bavaria in the Nazi era," the collaborative research project that Kershaw joined there) as an "inspirational mentor." He also declares that his close friendship with Hans Mommsen,* a leading historian of the period and another colleague on the project, provided a vital stimulus for his own work.[9] In particular, the concepts of resistance and consensus developed by the researchers on the project were extremely helpful when Kershaw came to formulate his own ideas on popular opinion and political dissent in the Third Reich, as well as on the role of Hitler himself.[10]

NOTES

1 See Mary Fulbrook, *German National Identity after the Holocaust* (Cambridge: Polity Press, 1999), esp. 103–25; also Mary Fulbrook, "German Historiography after 1945 Reconsidered," *Bulletin of the German Historical Institute London* 13, no. 1 (1991): 3–9.

2 "Geschichte des Instituts," accessed October 2015, http://www.ifz-muenchen.de/das-institut/ueber-das-institut/geschichte/.

3 Danny Millum, Interview with Ian Kershaw, May 14, 2008, accessed October 2015, http://www.history.ac.uk/makinghistory/resources/interviews/Kershaw_Ian.html.

4 See Ian Kershaw, *The "Hitler Myth": Image and Reality in the Third Reich* (Oxford: Oxford University Press, 2001), vii–viii.

5 David F. Crew, "*Alltagsgeschichte*: A New Social History 'From Below'?" *Central European History* 22, no. 3/4 (1989): 394–407, quotation from p. 395; see also Fulbrook, *German National Identity*, 118–21.

6 See Ian Kershaw, *The Nazi Dictatorship: Problems and Perspectives of Interpretation.* (London: Bloomsbury, 2000).

7 Johnpeter Horst Grill, "Local and Regional Studies on National Socialism: A Review," *Journal of Contemporary History* 21, no. 2 (1986): 253–94.

8 Millum, "Interview."

9 Ian Kershaw, "Beware the Moral High Ground," *Times Literary Supplement*, October 10, 2003.

10 Stephen Moss, "A Life in Writing: Ian Kershaw," *Guardian*, August 17, 2011.

MODULE 3
THE PROBLEM

KEY POINTS

- In writing *The "Hitler Myth"*, Ian Kershaw sought to engage with contemporary debates about how the Third Reich* and its crimes had been possible.

- Answers to this question were often polarized by arguments between "intentionalists,"* who portrayed Adolf Hitler as directly controlling all the Third Reich's policies, and "functionalists,"* who stressed the dictator's interaction with other competing power structures, such as the Nazi Party* and the SS,* which limited his scope for political action.

- In *The "Hitler Myth"*, Kershaw sought answers that went beyond these two competing camps of historical thought.

Core Question

Ian Kershaw's *The "Hitler Myth": Image and Reality in the Third Reich* addressed a question of particular and enduring concern to practitioners of the new "contemporary history" in West Germany (the Federal Republic of Germany)*: "How could Hitler happen?" How had the Third Reich—and all its attendant atrocities and barbarities—come to pass in a modern, civilized, Western European society? And who, ultimately, was to blame?

By addressing the problem of Adolf Hitler's rise and reign from the perspective of popular opinion, rather than taking the dictator himself as his starting point, Kershaw was setting *The "Hitler Myth"* up in opposition to what is known as the "Hitler Wave" of publications in the 1970s, which included a number of biographies and "psychohistorical"* studies of the Führer.* Psychohistory is an

> **❝** In the predominant West German historical picture, Nazism had more or less collided with the 'real' history of the German *Volk* [people], blowing it off course; the masses of the German people had been exposed to and blinded by Hitler's charms ... a criminal had taken over Germany ... and finally, after bitter defeat and division of the fatherland (the real catastrophe), the new West German state sought to rebuild on the ruins ... [Interpretations] served on the whole ... to exonerate the masses of the German people from any real responsibility for the Hitler regime. **❞**
>
> Mary Fulbrook, *German National Identity after the Holocaust*

approach that attempts to fuse insights from the therapeutic and theoretical method of psychoanalysis* with more traditional methods of historical inquiry, in order to explain the possible psychological motivations of historical figures. While guardedly praising the biography of Hitler written by the scholar Joachim Fest* from this period,[1] Kershaw himself critically described the "Hitler Wave" as "an outpouring of mainly worthless products ... indicating a macabre fascination with the bizarre personality of the Nazi leader ... [and often] adding little more than antiquarian detail to existing knowledge about Hitler."[2]

More broadly, Kershaw wished to avoid the prevalent "intentionalist" tendency to focus on the dictator as the root of all National Socialist (Nazi) evils. This model portrayed Hitler's personality, ideology, and strength of will as the utterly dominant force in the Third Reich. Above all, such theories depicted Hitler as pursuing a coherent ideological program from start to finish—a thesis that Kershaw found fundamentally unconvincing.[3]

The Participants

One of the key objections to this "intentionalist" model of ultimate Hitlerian power, which had primarily been put forward by scholars such as Karl Dietrich Bracher, Andreas Hillgruber,* Eberhard Jäckel,* and Klaus Hildebrand,* was that it absolved the German people more generally from any responsibility for Nazi crimes. It hardly seems coincidental that many of these historians were later so fully implicated in the *Historikerstreit* (Historians' Dispute) of 1986–7, in which they demanded a "normalization" and "relativization" of German crimes.[4] By contrast, other scholars, most notably Hans Mommsen* and Martin Broszat* at the *Institut für Zeitgeschichte* (Institute for Contemporary History)* in Munich, focused upon the competitive power dynamics and processes of "cumulative radicalization" inherent in the polycratic* structures of the Nazi state.[5] ("Polycratic" is a term denoting government by many rulers, commonly used to refer to the competing power structures within the Third Reich). Although they did not deny that Hitler's personal power was crucial to the functioning of the regime, these "functionalist" scholars argued that it was still just one element in a multi-layered structure of competing power bases, including Nazi Party bosses, SS leaders, and military commanders.[6]

These ideas were explored at length in Martin Broszat's book *The Hitler State*, first published in German in 1969.[7] However, by the early 1970s, Broszat had become more interested in exposing the Nazi state's underbelly, focusing on "history from below" rather than on "history from above." That is, he was concerned above all to determine, at a local level, how far all social classes and facets of society had been permeated by Nazism—partly in the hope of proving that there had been more grassroots resistance to the regime than had previously been supposed. This interest inspired him to set up and direct, from 1977 to 1983, a large-scale research project titled "Bavaria* under National Socialism," which would subsequently form the framework for Kershaw's research on *The "Hitler Myth"*.[8]

The Contemporary Debate

Kershaw's focus was necessarily influenced to some degree by his appointment as a researcher on the Bavarian research project at the Munich Institute for Contemporary History, and by the close contacts and friendships that he forged with other historians there.[9] Like his colleagues in Munich, Kershaw wished to escape both the politicized strictures of "totalitarianism theory,"* with its argument for equivalence between fascist and communist dictatorships, and the straitjacket of the "intentionalist versus functionalist" debate.[10]

From this perspective, an important piece in the intellectual jigsaw puzzle had already been contributed by Martin Broszat in an article on the German people's relationship with Hitler, which had been published in 1970 in the twentieth-anniversary edition of the Institute for Contemporary History's in-house journal, *Vierteljahrshefte für Zeitgeschichte* (Contemporary History Quarterly).*[11] Kershaw saw this piece as illuminating key interpretative problems of the Third Reich that Broszat's monumental book on *The Hitler State* had been unable to handle in any systematic way. In particular, it deepened scholarly understanding of the Nazi state as a political system, as well as linking the dictator unequivocally with the notion of charismatic leadership* proposed by the pioneering German sociologist* Max Weber.* "In my opinion," Kershaw writes, "the article should therefore be considered among [Broszat's] most important publications, controversial as it was at the time."[12]

NOTES

1 Joachim Fest, Hitler: *Eine Biographie* (Berlin: Propyläen Verlag, 1973).

2 Ian Kershaw, *The Nazi Dictatorship: Problems and Perspectives of Interpretation* (London: Bloomsbury, 2000), 71.

3 Kershaw, *The Nazi Dictatorship*, 70–4.

4   For more on this, see Charles Maier, *The Unmasterable Past: History, Holocaust, and German National Identity* (Cambridge, MA: Harvard University Press, 1988); Richard J. Evans, *In Hitler's Shadow: West German Historians and the Attempt to Escape from the Nazi Past* (New York: Pantheon, 1989).

5   For more on this, see their collected essays: Martin Broszat, *Nach Hitler: Der schwierige Umgang mit unserer Geschichte* (Munich: Oldenbourg, 1987); Hans Mommsen, *From Weimar to Auschwitz* (Princeton: Princeton University Press, 1991).

6   Kershaw, *The Nazi Dictatorship*, 74–9.

7   Martin Broszat, *Der Staat Hitlers: Grundlegung und Entwicklung seiner inneren Verfassung* (Munich: Deutscher Taschenbuch-Verlag, 1969).

8   On Broszat's inspiration and motivation, see Chris Lorenz, "Has the Third Reich become History? Martin Broszat as Historian and Pedagogue," *Bulletin of the Arnold and Leona Finkler Institute for Holocaust Research* 8 (1998): 27–44.

9   See Ian Kershaw, "Beware the Moral High Ground," *Times Literary Supplement*, October 10, 2003.

10 See Kershaw, *The Nazi Dictatorship*, 39, 92.

11 Martin Broszat, "Soziale Motivation und Führer-Bindung des Nationalsozialismus," *Vierteljahrshefte für Zeitgeschichte* 49 (1970): 392–409.

12 Ian Kershaw, "Soziale Motivation und Führer-Bindung im Staat Hitlers," in *Martin Broszat, der "Staat Hitlers" und die Historisierung des Nationalsozialismus*, ed. Norbert Frei (Göttingen: Wallstein, 2007), 76.

THE AUTHOR'S CONTRIBUTION

KEY POINTS

- In *The "Hitler Myth"*, Ian Kershaw aimed to illuminate the ways in which Adolf Hitler's image, fueled by propaganda,* was constructed and maintained through popular consent.

- Kershaw's work both established the idea of the "Hitler myth" as a key term in studies of the Third Reich* and linked the concept with Max Weber's* theory of charismatic leadership.*

- Kershaw's thought on Hitler was particularly indebted to the historian Martin Broszat's* article "Social Motivation and the Führer-Bond under National Socialism"* (1970).

Author's Aims

In *The "Hitler Myth": Image and Reality in the Third Reich*, Ian Kershaw aimed to clarify the reasons behind Adolf Hitler's adoration by "millions of Germans who might otherwise have been only marginally committed to Nazism.*"[1] After all, without Hitler's massive personal popularity, the regime could never have been sustained, or reached such murderous heights, for so long. However, Kershaw aimed to move beyond contemporary biographical and ideological explanations of the fascination that Hitler had exerted upon the German public. Rather than concentrating on the dictator* himself, Kershaw focused both on the propaganda process used to construct Hitler's image and, most importantly, on its popular reception. He defined the book as "a study in political imagery" that aimed "to demonstrate how the 'Hitler myth'—by which I mean a 'heroic' image and popular conception of Hitler imputing to him characteristics and motives for the most part at crass variance with

> ❝ The 'Hitler Myth' can be seen as providing the central
> motor for integration, mobilization and legitimation
> within the Nazi system of rule ... No one was more
> aware of the functional significance of his popularity in
> binding the masses to him ... than Hitler himself. ❞
>
> Ian Kershaw, *The "Hitler Myth": Image and Reality in the Third Riech*

reality—served its vital integratory function in providing the regime with its mass base of support."[2]

The structure of Kershaw's lucid analysis is broadly chronological. The first section begins with the genesis of the "Hitler myth" in the Weimar Republic* before charting Hitler's exponential rise in popularity during the years before World War II.* The second section then chronicles the (surprisingly slow) dissolution of Hitler's hold over the German people, as defeat in World War II began to loom ever closer. Separate chapters also consider public reactions to the Nazi Party and Hitler's relationship with the Christian Churches, while a final section considers the Hitler myth in relation to the "Jewish question"* (the racially charged debate on how Jewish minorities should be treated in German society).

Approach

Kershaw's coinage of the "Hitler myth" as a concept used both in the title of his book and throughout as a term of art* (that is, a term with a sense appropriate to a specific context) was to have a huge impact on all future discussions of Hitler's role in the Third Reich. Moreover, although Kershaw was not the first author to analyze Hitler's dictatorship in conjunction with the sociologist Max Weber's model of charismatic leadership, he was the first to popularize this model among historians of Nazi Germany.[3]

From another perspective, the broader framework provided by the historian Martin Broszat's Bavaria* project, including the sheer scale of the resources at its command, brought to light an invaluable amount of completely original primary sources that Kershaw would otherwise have been unable to use: "Doors were opened, and I was able to get access to material that was pouring out of local government offices. I went into several offices where the stuff hadn't even been delivered into the archives. It was just being brought out of the cellars, where it had languished since 1945. I was the first person to see it sometimes."[4]

This wealth of previously unresearched material, in conjunction with the new "bottom-up" approach to the history of the Third Reich that Broszat and his colleagues favored, provided the framework for Kershaw's unique fusion of *Alltagsgeschichte** ("history of everyday life") and completely original source analysis in the two books based on his research in Munich: *The "Hitler Myth"* and *Popular Opinion and Political Dissent in the Third Reich: Bavaria 1933–1945*.

Contribution in Context

It is useful here to consider the influence of the British historian Timothy Mason,* a specialist in the social history of the Third Reich. While Kershaw did not share Mason's socialist* standpoint, Mason's work seems to have contributed fundamentally to Kershaw's intellectual framework for *The "Hitler Myth"*. For example, Kershaw self-confessedly shared Mason's view that the sources of Hitler's popularity should be sought "in those who adored him, rather than in the leader himself."[5] Meanwhile, Kershaw's thesis that Hitler was eventually seduced by his own myth certainly has some basis in Mason's contention that "Hitler well understood his own function, the role which he *had* to act out as 'Leader' of the Third Reich."[6]

Both within the pages of *The "Hitler Myth"* and elsewhere, however, Kershaw has always emphasized above all the debt his work owes to Martin Broszat. Indeed, Broszat's influence had begun when Kershaw was still a medievalist, well before the two men had ever met, let alone begun working collaboratively as colleagues at the *Institut für Zeitgeschichte*

(Institute for Contemporary History)* in Munich.[7] Kershaw's initial impetus came from an article that Broszat had published in the journal *Vierteljahrshefte für Zeitgeschichte*,* "Social Motivation and the Führer-Bond under National Socialism."[8] It was in this article that the idea of the Führer* as a charismatic figure, embodying the diverse desires of an otherwise rather chaotic movement, and uniting them in radical utopianism, was first mooted ("utopianism" here refers to Hitler's pursuit of an impossible social ideal). Broszat's focus on what Hitler *symbolized*, as opposed to his concrete actions, provided the key that would later unlock the potential for Kershaw's own analysis.[9]

NOTES

1   Ian Kershaw, *The "Hitler Myth": Image and Reality in the Third Reich* (Oxford: Oxford University Press, 2001), 1.

2   Kershaw, *"Hitler Myth"*, 2–3.

3   For an example of an earlier work that used this interpretative framework, see Joseph Nyomarkay, *Charisma and Factionalism within the Nazi Party* (Minneapolis: University of Minnesota Press, 1967).

4   Stephen Moss, "A Life in Writing: Ian Kershaw," *Guardian*, August 17, 2011.

5   Timothy W. Mason, "Open Questions on Nazism," in *People's History and Socialist Theory*, ed. Rupert Samuel (London: Routledge, 1981), 207, with citation in Kershaw, *"Hitler Myth"*, 2.

6   Timothy W. Mason, "Intention and Explanation: A Current Controversy about the Interpretation of National Socialism," in *Der 'Führerstaat'. Mythos und Realität. Studien zur Struktur und Politik des Dritten Reiches*, eds. Gerhard Hirschfeld and Lothar Kettenacker (Stuttgart: Klett-Cotta,1981), 35, with citation in Kershaw, *"Hitler Myth"*, 3.

7   Ian Kershaw, "Soziale Motivation und Führer-Bindung im Staat Hitlers," in *Martin Broszat, der "Staat Hitlers" und die Historisierung des Nationalsozialismus*, ed. Norbert Frei (Göttingen: Wallstein, 2007), 76.

8   Martin Broszat, "Soziale Motivation und Führer-Bindung des Nationalsozialismus," *Vierteljahrshefte für Zeitgeschichte* 49 (1970): 392–409. On charismatic leadership, see particularly pp. 401ff.

9   See Kershaw, *"Hitler Myth"*, vii; Kershaw, "Soziale Motivation," 76.

SECTION 2
IDEAS

MODULE 5
MAIN IDEAS

KEY POINTS

- *The "Hitler Myth"* aims to show how popular perceptions of Adolf Hitler, shaped by propaganda,* mobilized the German people in support of the Nazi* regime.

- Hitler's propaganda-fueled image as a caring, peace-loving leader tended to bear very little resemblance to the reality of his belligerent intentions.

- Despite being initially—and primarily—intended for an academic audience, *The "Hitler Myth"* is engagingly written and highly readable.

Key Themes

Put simply, Ian Kershaw's *The "Hitler Myth": Image and Reality in the Third Reich* argues that Adolf Hitler's propaganda-fueled image functioned to bind together the potentially divisive forces within the Nazi movement, mobilizing both the Nazi Party faithful and the broader mass of "non-organized" Germans. In the German popular imagination, the dictator* was refashioned as a "fictive figure, manufactured by propaganda on the foundations of pre-existing heroic leadership ideals"—even though this mythical Hitler bore next to no resemblance to the man himself.[1] Thus, the figure of Hitler was seen as a personification of the nation, divorced from all the petty corruptions of Party officials. Moreover, the dictator was personally given credit for all the regime's successes—whether in the realm of economics (with the reduction of unemployment) or in foreign policy (with German military rearmament and the annexation of the Rhineland,* actions that overturned the harsh terms of the Treaty of Versailles,* a profoundly resented peace treaty concluding World War I).*

> **❝** There were still many Germans who were skeptical of Hitler when he became chancellor in 1933. But Führer propaganda and military success soon turned him into an idol. The adulation helped make the Third Reich catastrophe possible. **❞**
>
> Ian Kershaw, "The Führer Myth: How Hitler Won Over the German People," *Spiegel Online International*

In the run-up to World War II,* Hitler was hailed as a statesman of genius, "an upholder and fanatical defender of Germany's rights … not as a racial imperialist* warmonger working toward a 'war of annihilation' and limitless German conquest"[2] ("imperialist" here denotes someone engaged, quite simply, in empire building). He was also seen as Germany's sole savior and protector—both practically, in terms of his unparalleled military leadership, and ideologically, in terms of his crusade against the twin evils of Bolshevism* and the perceived economic and political influence of Jewish people.* The myth only started to lose its hold when Germany's military defeat began to seem inevitable, though some of its elements even remained alive in the German imagination after the war's end in 1945.

Exploring the Ideas

One of the most fascinating (and ironic) elements of the "Hitler myth" was the chronic mismatch between the dictator's benevolent popular image and the reality of his brutal intentions. The German people greeted many of Hitler's foreign policy successes with such jubilation precisely because they had seemingly spared Germany from becoming embroiled in another global conflict. After all, the brutality and mass slaughter of World War I and its aftermath was still fresh in popular memory. So when Hitler managed to achieve the annexation first of the Rhineland, then of Austria (a forced union known as the "*Anschluss*"),* and finally the incorporation of the Czech

Sudetenland* region into German territory, all without triggering a new military conflagration, people's overwhelming fear of war was transformed into a mixture of euphoric relief and genuine admiration for the dictator's achievements. Had they known that Hitler's ultimate goal was deliberately to provoke a conflict, and that, following the Munich Agreement*—in which the international community forced Czechoslovakia to cede the Sudetenland to Germany without a fight—he was "furious at being maneuvered into a diplomatic settlement of the question," their fervor might have been somewhat subdued.[3] As it was, when war was declared in 1939, many Germans genuinely believed that Hitler had done his best for peace, even if they did not greet the news with any great enthusiasm.[4] In more general terms, by the time of his 50th birthday on September 20, 1939, "the great majority of Germans could find some point of identification with Hitler and his 'achievements.'"[5]

Language and Expression

In stylistic terms, *The "Hitler Myth"* occupies a middle ground between specialist academic prose and a more popular or journalistic idiom. Each chapter tends to be headed by a couple of epigraphs (pertinent lines of text, commonly quotations) that illustrate some of the following section's key points. The argument is carefully signposted throughout, with the connections between chapters often highlighted in their concluding or opening paragraphs. The frequent quotations from original sources, often featuring the voices of ordinary German people, and Kershaw's highly engaging way with words, make the book a most rewarding read. Take, for example, the following passage: "At the Reich Party Rally in 1936 [Hitler] now spoke himself of a mystical unity between himself and the German people: 'That you have found me … among so many miracles is the miracle of our time! And that I have found you, that is Germany's fortune!' All the signs are that this was no longer pure rhetoric. Hitler himself was a convert to the 'Führer* myth', himself a 'victim' of Nazi propaganda … What seems certain is that the day on which Hitler started to believe in his own 'myth' marked in a sense the beginning of the end of the Third Reich."[6]

As well as showcasing his prose style, this passage clearly demonstrates Kershaw's ability to identify and focus upon key moments and pieces of evidence that support his theory; the two are then skillfully interwoven to form a colorful tapestry of original evidence and striking analysis.

NOTES

1 Ian Kershaw, *The "Hitler Myth": Image and Reality in the Third Reich* (Oxford: Oxford University Press, 2001), 253. An excellent overview of Kershaw's main strands of argument can be found on pp. 253–60.

2 Kershaw, *"Hitler Myth"*, 253–4.

3 Kershaw, *"Hitler Myth"*, 138.

4 See Kershaw, *"Hitler Myth"*, 121–47.

5 Kershaw, *"Hitler Myth"*, 140–1.

6 Kershaw, *"Hitler Myth"*, 82.

MODULE 6
SECONDARY IDEAS

KEY POINTS

- In *The "Hitler Myth"*, Ian Kershaw argued that Adolf Hitler's* personal popularity often grew at the expense of the popularity of the Nazi Party.* He also argued that the Christian Churches often believed that Hitler would protect them—particularly from Nazi fanatics who were belligerently antireligious. In fact, Hitler's personal attitude to the Churches was equally hostile.

- In general, popular opinion in Nazi Germany tended to suppose that Hitler was completely ignorant of the problems caused by his Party subordinates, and that he would act swiftly to temper their excesses, if only he knew about them.

- Other German historians swiftly took up many of Kershaw's ideas—particularly his chronological account of the rise and fall of the "Hitler myth."

Other Ideas

Although the structure of *The "Hitler Myth": Image and Reality in the Third Reich* is broadly chronological, Ian Kershaw explores a number of subsidiary ideas in chapters that stand to some extent outside this framework. Thus, in chapter 3, "'Führer without Sin': Hitler and the 'little Hitlers,'" Kershaw argues that Hitler's personality cult actually grew at the expense of the Nazi Party itself. In order to support his argument, Kershaw focuses on two case studies.

First, he analyzes public reactions to Hitler's purge of the higher ranks of the SA (*Sturmabteilung*),* the Nazi paramilitary organization, and its leader Ernst Röhm,* in July 1934 (the so-called Night of the Long Knives).* Members of the SA were supposedly plotting a coup

> ❝ I must counter here … the cliché so often heard, especially among the bourgeoisie: 'Yes, the Führer*— but the Party, that's a different matter!' To that I give the answer: 'No, gentlemen, the Führer is the Party and the Party is the Führer. ❞
>
> Adolf Hitler, Nuremberg Party Rally, 1935

against Hitler, while also routinely engaging in homosexual exploits that Nazi ideology deemed to be criminal and depraved.

Second, Kershaw looks at popular reactions to the actions of local Nazi Party bosses, whose corruptibility and brutality often irrevocably tarnished the Party's image, while simultaneously burnishing the Hitler myth. The public was often convinced that "the Führer would intervene decisively if he once got wind of the daily abuses of his underlings."[1]

In chapter 4, "The Führer versus the Radicals: Hitler's Image and the 'Church Struggle,'" meanwhile, Kershaw argues that Hitler was often viewed, even by Church leaders, as a staunch defender of religious values—protecting the Christian Churches both against godless Bolshevism* and, perhaps even more importantly, against the relentlessly antireligious ideological fanatics of the Nazi movement.[2] There was a widespread "unwillingness to believe that the Führer himself could be lying in his professions of support for the Churches."[3] In both cases, it seems that the German people desperately needed to believe in the secular (that is, nonreligious) redemption and national salvation that the "Hitler myth" seemed to offer.

Exploring the Ideas

As in the case of foreign policy and the build-up to war, the inverse relationship of the Party's popularity to Hitler's own popularity, and the goodwill credited to him by the Churches, were also intimately connected with public ignorance of the dictator's* true intentions. So the "Night of the Long Knives," when the SA leadership was assassinated at Hitler's request, was a perfect propaganda-fed coup precisely because the German people were kept completely in the dark about the real political motives behind the slaughter. While Hitler had killed Ernst Röhm and his associates because he feared their creating a rival power base, popular opinion commended him for rooting out rot, decadence, and debauchery within the Party. The purge was greeted with loud approval, and some people even expressed hope that further purges might occur in the future. Kershaw suggests that this may have occurred because "the propaganda portrayal of Hitler as the upholder of moral standards corresponded closely with commonly-held social values and prejudices in its condemnation of venal corruption and homosexuality."[4] Hitler's action was deemed the strong, brave deed of a true leader, and the fact that it was beyond the bounds of legality was seen as strength rather than criminality—anything to avoid further revolutionary bloodshed and upheaval.[5]

The purge also perpetuated the myth that when Hitler failed to act to curb excesses and evils among his subordinates, this was simply because he had not yet discovered the truth about them. Meanwhile, the upstart "little Hitler" Party bigwigs who started throwing their weight around bore the brunt of popular dissatisfaction with the necessarily imperfect reality of life after the Nazi "revolution." Local leaders' "corrupt catering for [elite] self-interest" revealed that the Nazi Party was just as bad as any other political party. Still, it was hoped that Hitler, as a "righteous authority," would move to curb these ills as soon as he was informed about them, just as he had swiftly removed Röhm and his fellow "conspirators."[6]

Overlooked

The "Hitler Myth" found a wide audience from the start, and many of its ideas quickly gained wider resonance—for instance, Kershaw's depiction of the broad chronological development of Hitler's propaganda-fueled image, or the notion that, at least by the beginning of World War II,* the dictator had actually begun to believe in his own myth.[7] However, not all of the arguments in *The "Hitler Myth"* were to become authoritative quite so quickly. To some extent, articles that he had already published on the subject overshadowed the ideas in Kershaw's final chapter on "Hitler's Popular Image and the 'Jewish Question.'" Furthermore, the chapter was only added to the second, English edition, published in 1987, rather than being included in the first, German-language version of the work, which had appeared in 1980.[8] Less attention was also paid to the detailed scene-setting of the origins of Hitler's image in the Weimar Republic,* which Kershaw discussed in depth in the first chapter of *The "Hitler Myth."* Here, Kershaw drew attention to the debt that Hitler owed both to Italian fascism* and the cult of the Italian fascist leader Mussolini,* and also to failed attempts during Germany's imperial period to promote the monarch, Kaiser Wilhelm II,* as the "People's Emperor."[9]

NOTES

1   Ian Kershaw, *The "Hitler Myth": Image and Reality in the Third Reich* (Oxford: Oxford University Press, 2001), 83–104; quotation from p. 104.

2   Kershaw, *"Hitler Myth"*, 105–20.

3   Kershaw, *"Hitler Myth"*, 120.

4   Kershaw, *"Hitler Myth"*, 92.

5   Kershaw, *"Hitler Myth"*, 84–95.

6   Kershaw, *"Hitler Myth"*, 103–4.

7   For examples of these notions being more widely popularized, see David Nicholls, *Adolf Hitler: A Biographical Companion* (Oxford: ABC-CLIO, 2000), 121–3; Laurence Rees, *The Dark Charisma of Adolf Hitler: Leading Millions into the Abyss* (London: Ebury Press, 2013), 130.

8   For criticism along these lines, see Jürgen Matthäus, *"Hitler, the Germans, and the Final Solution,"* by Ian Kershaw, *Central European History* 42, no. 3 (2009): 582–4.

9   See Kershaw, *"Hitler Myth"*, 13–17, 21–2.

MODULE 7
ACHIEVEMENT

KEY POINTS

- In *The "Hitler Myth"*, Ian Kershaw successfully realized his aim of illuminating how the Nazi* regime functioned by focusing on how ordinary Germans viewed Adolf Hitler,* and how their perspectives changed over time.

- Revising the book for an English-speaking audience, while taking account of new material from archives in German regions other than Bavaria and new research on Hitler and the genocidal* event known as the Holocaust,* enabled *The "Hitler Myth"* to gain worldwide acclaim.

- The book was sometimes criticized, however, for being undertheorized and for lacking definitions for key concepts such as "political myth."

Assessing the Argument

In writing *The "Hitler Myth": Image and Reality in the Third Reich*, Ian Kershaw's professed aim had been "to make a modest contribution to an understanding of the dynamics of National Socialist* [Nazi] rule by looking at the way—mirrored through a great many reports on popular opinion compiled by agents of the regime at numerous levels—ordinary people viewed Hitler during the Third Reich.*"[1]

In many ways, Kershaw certainly managed to achieve his goal, providing a lucid and engaging chronological and thematic account of the development of the "Hitler myth" and its reception, including the dictator's* seduction by his own propaganda machine. Although *The "Hitler Myth"* did not escape criticism entirely when it first appeared, either in German in 1980, or in English in 1987, its importance and originality were nevertheless widely acknowledged. For example, Jay

> ❝ Ian Kershaw describes popular perceptions of Hitler and the propagandistic efforts that went into the making of Hitler's image. His sources are primarily from Bavaria—where some of the richest and most diversified materials on public opinion have survived—and they are densest for the period between 1930 and 1941. The study ... lacks theory and conceptualization. However, the author is thoroughly familiar with his sources, he knows their potentials and limits, and it is a delight following him in showing the patterns and shifts in public opinion. It is a remarkable, well-balanced and even-handed undertaking. ❞
>
> Michael Geyer, "Der Hitler-Mythos: Volksmeinung und Propaganda im Dritten Reich," by Ian Kershaw, *Journal of Modern History*

W. Baird began his critique for the *American Historical Review* by declaring, "Ian Kershaw has written an important book."[2]

However, it is worth noting that some of Kershaw's most influential ideas—such as his analysis of the "Hitler myth" through the lens of the sociologist* Max Weber's* theory of "charismatic leadership,"* and the third section of the book in its entirety, entitled "The 'Hitler Myth' and the Path to Genocide"—were later additions that had never existed at all in the original German edition, entitled *Der Hitler-Mythos: Volksmeinung und Propaganda im Dritten Reich*. Thus, Kershaw's thought on the topic essentially remained fluid and to some extent incomplete until he had eventually managed to produce the (substantially revised) English edition of the work.

Achievement in Context

In its first, German, incarnation, which appeared as part of a series published by the *Institut für Zeitgeschichte* (Institute for Contemporary

History)* in Munich in 1980, *The "Hitler Myth"* did not gain a very broad readership beyond the German-speaking world.[3] Although Kershaw stressed that "the kind reception of the book, quite especially in Germany, suggested that I was along the right lines, and gave me a good deal of satisfaction," his ideas were only to gain a truly worldwide impact once the book's first English edition had been published by Oxford University Press in 1987.[4]

One problem that Kershaw felt the need to remedy in the English edition, and which some reviewers had commented upon at the outset, was the geographically restricted nature of his sources.[5] Because his research had been carried out as part of the historian Martin Broszat's* grand research project on "Bavaria under National Socialism," most of Kershaw's original source material necessarily came from archives in Bavaria alone.[6] But were his findings really applicable throughout the Third Reich, given Germany's strongly differentiated federal and regional character?

In order to counter potential criticism on this score, Kershaw widened his net accordingly, visiting further archives throughout Germany in order to "[dilute] the concentration on Bavaria in the original version."[7] He then systematically overhauled and updated the English text to incorporate his new findings.[8] This new version of the book was so successful that it was republished without any further updating in German in 1999, even though the field had by now moved on considerably.[9]

Limitations

As soon as *The "Hitler Myth"* was first published, other scholars were aware of the potential it might have to illuminate other areas of history—or even other disciplines—even if they did not necessarily feel that this potential had yet been fully realized. Accordingly, in an early review of the German edition, the historian Michael Geyer* suggested that, although "it is quite obvious that a lot of work still needs to be done," Kershaw's analysis could usefully be augmented with "some of the ideas and analytical tools that are common in anthropology,* cultural studies,* or semiotics*" (anthropology is the study of humankind, commonly conducted through inquiry into culture and belief; cultural studies is a politically oriented field of inquiry drawing on the aims and methods of many different academic fields; semiotics is the study of the ways in which meaning is transmitted through signs, notably in language). He concluded by commenting that, from this perspective, "Kershaw's perceptive study leads us in the right direction."[10]

Geyer also mentioned a point that other reviewers, particularly in Germany, would subsequently take issue with: the fact that the book was in no way theory-driven, and that the concepts developed within it were often left without a hard and fast definition.[11] A review of several of Kershaw's works, published shortly after the revised German edition of *Der Hitler-Mythos* had appeared in 1999, went much further, castigating the work for the "methodological deficits" that it contained: "Kershaw does not supply a firm definition of the political myth, nor does he analyze its propagandistic construction more precisely." The reviewer also complained that Kershaw had made no attempt to take account of regional differences, "whether between town and country, northern and southern Germany, etc."[12]

Meanwhile, Kershaw himself has warned of the danger of making overly general comparisons based upon his work on the Third Reich. In response to an interviewer who asked him whether he saw "similarities between the Europe of the 1930s and the continent today, with economic collapse, alienation from the political class and scapegoating of minorities," he replied that another 1933 seemed "a distant prospect," and that one should beware of "generalizing from this one tragedy."[13]

NOTES

1   Ian Kershaw, *The "Hitler Myth": Image and Reality in the Third Reich* (Oxford: Oxford University Press, 2001), vii.

2   Jay W. Baird, *"The 'Hitler Myth': Image and Reality in the Third Reich,"* by Ian Kershaw *American Historical Review* 95, no. 5 (1990): 1569.

3   Ian Kershaw, *Der Hitler-Mythos: Volksmeinung und Propaganda im Dritten Reich (Schriftenreihe der Vierteljahrshefte für Zeitgeschichte;* Stuttgart: Deutsche Verlags-Anstalt, 1980).

4   Kershaw, *"Hitler Myth"*, vii.

5   See for example Michael Geyer, *"Der Hitler-Mythos: Volksmeinung und Propaganda im Dritten Reich"* by Ian Kershaw, *Journal of Modern History 54*, no. 4 (1982): 811.

6   Kershaw, *"Hitler Myth"*, viii–xi.

7   Kershaw, *"Hitler Myth"*, viii.

8   Kershaw, *"Hitler Myth"*, viii–xi, 274–6.

9   Ian Kershaw, *Der Hitler-Mythos: Führerkult und Volksmeinung* (Stuttgart: Deutsche Verlags-Anstalt, 1999). For criticism of Kershaw's failure to update this new German edition further, see Michael Wildt, "'Wenn das der Führer wüßte.' Ian Kershaw über Entstehung und Wirkung des Hitler-Mythos," *Die Zeit*, March 30, 2000.

10 Geyer, *"Der Hitler-Mythos,"* 812.

11 Geyer, *"Der Hitler-Mythos,"* 811.

12 Jens Hacke, "Sammelrez: Ian Kershaw: Der Hitler-Mythos," H-Soz-Kult, November 30, 2000, accessed November 2015, https://www.h-net.org/reviews/showpdf.php?id=18575.

13 Stephen Moss, "A Life in Writing: Ian Kershaw," *Guardian*, August 17, 2011.

MODULE 8
PLACE IN THE AUTHOR'S WORK

KEY POINTS

- *The "Hitler Myth"* represents the beginning of Ian Kershaw's long-standing interest in Adolf Hitler's* power and charisma, providing a springboard for his later best-selling Hitler biographies, and other works on the Third Reich.*

- The book was Kershaw's first work of modern history; previously, his research had focused on the medieval history of British monasteries.

- *The "Hitler Myth"* established Kershaw as a respected scholar in his new field of modern German history, both in the English-speaking world and in Germany.

Positioning

In its original German incarnation, published in 1980 as *Der Hitler-Mythos: Volksmeinung und Propaganda im Dritten Reich*, Ian Kershaw's *The "Hitler Myth": Image and Reality in the Third Reich* represented his first major foray into modern German history. As he comments wryly in the preface to the latest English edition, this made "quite a change from my previous work on monastic economy in England in the thirteenth and fourteenth centuries."[1] Along with the other book based on his research at Munich's *Institut für Zeitgeschichte* (Institute for Contemporary History),* *Popular Opinion and Political Dissent in the Third Reich* (1983), *The "Hitler Myth"* arguably laid crucial foundations for all of Kershaw's numerous future studies of Nazi* Germany.[2] In particular, it provided the basis for his later sustained engagement with "the social history of Hitler,"[3] beginning with a brief sketch entitled *Hitler: A Profile in Power* (1991), and continuing with his monumental

> ❝ I had at the time no special interest in Hitler himself.
> Rather, I had intended to deal with varying aspects
> of popular opinion in Bavaria, primarily a number of
> spheres of political dissent. At the same time, I became
> struck by the way the public image of Hitler repeatedly
> seemed to figure in the reports I was studying ...
> Though I did not realize it at the time, it was to be the
> start of a path that took me over the best part of two
> decades ever closer to the Dictator himself. ❞
>
> Ian Kershaw, *The "Hitler Myth"*: Image and Reality in the Third Reich

two-volume biography of the Führer,* *Hitler, 1889–1936: Hubris*
(1998) and *Hitler, 1936–1946: Nemesis* (2000).[4]

Although the biography was obviously more concerned with
Adolf Hitler as a historical actor in his own right than as an abstract
symbol, commentators often mentioned the significance of *The "Hitler
Myth"* and its key concepts for Kershaw's later approach to the
dictator's life.[5] Meanwhile, the new chapter on "Hitler's Popular Image
and the 'Jewish Question'", which Kershaw included in the first
English edition of *The "Hitler Myth"* (1987), also drew on his
burgeoning interest in the origins of the Holocaust,* on which he had
already published several important articles.[6]

Integration

As one interviewer once asked Kershaw, "I believe you used to be a
professor in medieval history. So how come you've gone on to
specialize in contemporary history and the issue of Nazism?"[7]
Kershaw's work on the Third Reich certainly follows a coherent
trajectory, beginning with explorations of popular opinion, moving
on to public perceptions of Hitler, and then considering the life of the
dictator himself, as well as the power structures within which he

operated. But how does any of that connect with his previous research on the economic habits of medieval monks in Bolton Priory?*[8]

The historian and social scientist John Breuilly,* formerly Kershaw's colleague at the University of Manchester, suggests that Kershaw's wide range of interests has ultimately contributed greater depth to his analyses of the Nazi dictatorship: "When he writes of charismatic authority in relation to Hitler he also knows about how princely power worked in medieval Europe. When he expresses skepticism about the fashionable idea of National Socialism [Nazism] as 'political religion' he does so as someone who has closely studied religious institutions … and deeply Christian societies."[9] Occasionally, Kershaw also draws specific links between the two periods in which he has specialized—for instance, likening the actions of fanatical fans of the Führer who were desperate to possess objects that Hitler had touched to the quasi-religious superstition of peasants who believed in "the supposed healing qualities of the touch of medieval monarchs."[10]

Significance

When questioned about his life's work, Kershaw tends not to dwell on *The "Hitler Myth"*, focusing instead on books such as *The Nazi Dictatorship: Problems and Perspectives of Interpretation* (1985), or the Hitler biographies.[11] Certainly, it was the popular impact of *Hubris* and *Nemesis*, rather than his earlier academic texts, that ultimately launched his career as a global superstar historian. Still, along with his concept of "working towards the Führer" and his pithy observation that the road to the concentration camp* Auschwitz*—the site of well over a million murders—was "built by hate, but paved with indifference," the "Hitler myth" swiftly became a defining concept in the scholarly canon (that is, authoritative body of works) on the Third Reich.[12] Kershaw himself stated in the preface to the 2001 edition that he was "delighted with the resonance of the book … Though, of course, research has moved on in important ways since 1987, my feeling is that the findings of my research as I presented them then have generally stood the test of time."[13] Even his more recent best sellers aimed primarily at a popular audience, including *Making Friends with Hitler* (2004), *Fateful Choices* (2007), and *The End* (2011), arguably owe a large debt to his initial explorations of Hitler's charismatic and symbolic power.[14] Meanwhile, as an academic at the very beginning of his modern historical career, it was *The "Hitler Myth"* that first made Kershaw's name as an expert to be reckoned with in both the English-speaking and German scholarly communities.

NOTES

1   Ian Kershaw, *The "Hitler Myth": Image and Reality in the Third Reich* (Oxford: Oxford University Press, 2001), vii.

2   Ian Kershaw, *Popular Opinion and Political Dissent in the Third Reich: Bavaria 1933–1945* (Oxford: Oxford University Press, 1983); see also Ian Kershaw, *The Nazi Dictatorship: Problems and Perspectives of Interpretation* (London: Bloomsbury, 2000).

3   Ian Kershaw, *Hitler, the Germans, and the Final Solution* (New Haven: Yale University Press, 2008), 59.

4   Ian Kershaw, *Hitler: A Profile in Power* (London: Longman, 1991); Ian Kershaw, *Hitler, 1889–1936: Hubris* (London: Penguin, 1998); Ian Kershaw, *Hitler, 1936–1946: Nemesis* (London: Penguin, 2000). Penguin also recently condensed the two volumes into an abridged single-volume version to appeal to a wider readership.

5   See, for instance, reviews of Kershaw, *Nemesis*, by Henry Ashby Turner, *Journal of Modern History* 75, no. 1 (2003): 214–15, and Bernard Wasserstein, *English Historical Review* 118, no. 475 (2003): 162–3; also Irene Kacandes, "Klaus L. Berghahn and Jost Hermand, eds., *Unmasking Hitler: Cultural Representations of Hitler from the Weimar Republic to the Present*," *German Quarterly* 80, no. 4 (2007): 545.

6   For a collection of his essays on this topic, see Kershaw, *Hitler, the Germans, and the Final Solution*.

7   Thomas Roman, "Interview with Ian Kershaw," *Eurozine*, October 24, 2002, accessed October 2015, http://www.eurozine.com/articles/2002-10-24-roman-en.html.

8   Ian Kershaw, *Bolton Priory: The Economy of a Northern Monastery, 1268–1325* (Oxford: Oxford University Press, 1973).

9   John Breuilly, "Personal Reflections on Ian Kershaw," in *Working Towards the Führer: Essays in Honour of Sir Ian Kershaw*, eds. Anthony McElligott and Tim Kirk (Manchester: Manchester University Press, 2004), 261.

10 Kershaw, *"Hitler Myth"*, 30–31.

11 See for instance Danny Millum, interview with Ian Kershaw, May 14, 2008, accessed October 2015, http://www.history.ac.uk/makinghistory/resources/interviews/Kershaw_Ian.html; Stephen Moss, "A Life in Writing: Ian Kershaw," *Guardian*, August 17, 2011.

12 Jürgen Matthäus, "*Hitler, the Germans, and the Final Solution* by Ian Kershaw," *Central European History* 42, no. 3 (2009): 582.

13 Kershaw, *"Hitler Myth"*, ix.

14 Ian Kershaw, *Making Friends with Hitler: Lord Londonderry and Britain's Road to War* (London: Penguin, 2004); Ian Kershaw, *Fateful Choices: Ten Decisions that Changed the World, 1940–1941* (London: Penguin, 2007); Ian Kershaw, *The End: Hitler's Germany, 1944–45* (London: Penguin, 2011).

SECTION 3
IMPACT

MODULE 9
THE FIRST RESPONSES

KEY POINTS

- While initial reception of The "Hitler Myth" tended to be positive, some reviewers felt that the book lacked originality and theoretical sophistication. They also questioned Kershaw's assumptions about popular responses to the "Jewish question."*

- Kershaw tended not to engage publicly with such criticisms; rather, his conception of the "Hitler myth" remained relatively stable over the coming decades.

- The only major changes to Kershaw's argument occurred when he reworked the initial German version of the book for publication in English during the mid-1980s.

Criticism

When The "Hitler Myth": Image and Reality in the Third Reich was first published, both in English and in German, the response was generally highly favorable. Leading scholars in the field variously described the book as "important," "immensely readable," and "a delight."[1]

Nevertheless, three main types of criticism were discernible. First, some scholars were skeptical about how original Ian Kershaw's English edition from 1987 really was, when it was "not so much a 'new book' … as a translation enriched with previously printed findings." One historian even went on to damn the work with faint praise: "Now even if originality cannot reasonably be said to constitute a major feature … it is still a very useful book to have on the shelf."[2]

Others challenged the sophistication of the theoretical framework that Kershaw used to underpin his argument. The reviewers in question disputed his use of terms such as "myth" and "charisma," or

> ❝ We know the outcome of Hitler's rule and it needs great imagination to understand how the 'Hitler myth' could ever have been believed. Ian Kershaw's self-imposed task is to discover how this 'Hitler Myth', so obviously a complete inversion of reality, was created and why it was so eagerly accepted. The result is a fascinating, meticulously researched, excellently written and thought-provoking study which skillfully avoids the pitfalls of a crass 'Hitlerocentrism' and an equally absurd depersonalization of the history of the Third Reich. ❞ *
>
> Martin Kitchen, *"The 'Hitler Myth': Image and Reality in the Third Reich by Ian Kershaw," Social History*

argued that he did not differentiate enough according to social group: "Though Kershaw does discuss differences in perception of Hitler where a political subculture is concerned (Catholics,* Socialists*), and there are scattered references to 'conservative elites,' the analysis could be much more systematic."[3]

Finally, Kershaw's treatment of Adolf Hitler and the "Jewish question" was not universally accepted, particularly his idea that "the large majority of Germans was attracted to Hitler and his movement not because of any 'Jewish' issue, but for other reasons."[4] On these grounds, one reviewer attacked Kershaw explicitly for his perceived insensitivity to "the problem of the 'Final Solution'"* (the systematic extermination of all of Europe's Jews).[5]

However, when reviewers did criticize Kershaw's work, they tended to frame their negative comments within an overall assessment that was generally extremely positive. The scholarly consensus seemed to be that, small gripes notwithstanding, Kershaw had made a valuable contribution to scholarship on the Third Reich.

Responses

Given the generally positive tone of the book's reception, both in German and in English, Kershaw seems to have felt little need to engage directly with his critics in the public sphere. After all, his work had no explicitly political intent—for the most part, it simply aimed to engage with scholarly debates about the nature of the Nazi regime; presumably, he saw no point in taking particular issue with those assessments of his work that took a slightly more negative tone.

When Kershaw did publish popular treatments of the subject, these tended simply to summarize his findings, rather than providing a forum for self-defense. One might contrast this with other scholars, such as Timothy Snyder, who works in similar areas of twentieth-century European history, but has often used media appearances to defend his work against criticism.[6] Over a span of approximately three decades, Kershaw's conception of the "Hitler myth" seems to have remained remarkably stable, as borne out by two popularizing articles, the first published in the British journal *History Today* in 1985, and the second in the German periodical *Spiegel Online International* in 2008.[7] The fact that Kershaw saw no need to make further changes to the substance of *The "Hitler Myth"*, leaving the text of both the 1999 German edition and the 2001 English edition exactly "as I left it in 1987,"[8] apart from a number of additions to the bibliography, also implies his general satisfaction with his theories in their original form.[9]

Conflict and Consensus

Nevertheless, Kershaw did take account of his critics—both potential and actual—during his substantial revision of the original German edition of *Der Hitler-Mythos*, which had been published in 1980, for publication in English. In particular, he acknowledged the previously very "Bavaria*-centric" nature of his source material, seeking out supplementary sources in archives further afield to broaden the general applicability of his thesis. Moreover, by supplying a new theoretical framework for his analysis of Hitler's symbolic hold over the German people, in the form of Max Weber's* sociological* model of "charismatic leadership,"* Kershaw may in part have been hoping to counter the criticism put forward by scholars such as Michael Geyer,* who, despite being fundamentally impressed with *Der Hitler-Mythos*, depicted the book as somewhat lacking in theoretical coherence.[10]

Finally, we might wonder whether Kershaw's renewed engagement with Hitler in his later biographical studies of the dictator,* which fused the concept of the "Hitler myth" with other original ideas, such as the notion of "working towards the Führer," might have been partly prompted by a desire to prove that he could still contribute new ideas to the debate on Hitler's power, while simultaneously trumping those scholars who had criticized the English edition of *The "Hitler Myth"* for its lack of originality.

NOTES

1 Jay W. Baird, *"The 'Hitler Myth': Image and Reality in the Third Reich* by Ian Kershaw," *American Historical Review* 95, no. 5 (1990): 1569; John P. Fox, "*The Ideological Origins of Nazi Imperialism* by Woodruff D. Smith and *The 'Hitler Myth': Image and Reality in the Third Reich* by Ian Kershaw," *International Affairs* 64, no. 2 (1988): 293; Michael Geyer, "*Der Hitler-Mythos: Volksmeinung und Propaganda im Dritten Reich* by Ian Kershaw," *Journal of Modern History* 54, no. 4 (1982): 811.

2 Michael H. Kater. *"The 'Hitler Myth': Image and Reality in the Third Reich* by Ian Kershaw," *English Historical Review* 103, no. 409 (1988): 1014; see also Fox, *"Ideological Origins,"* 293.

3 David F. Lindenfeld, *"The 'Hitler Myth': Image and Reality in the Third Reich by Ian Kershaw,"* *German Studies Review* 11, no. 2 (1988): 329; Geyer, *"Der Hitler-Mythos,"* 812.

4 Kater, *"The 'Hitler Myth,'"* 1016.

5 Baird, "*The 'Hitler Myth,'"* 1569.

6   See, for example, Timothy Snyder, "In Defense of *Bloodlands*," *Tablet*, August 3, 2012, accessed November 2015, http://www.tabletmag.com/jewish-arts-and-culture/books/108229/in-defense-of-bloodlands.

7   See Ian Kershaw, "The Hitler Myth," *History Today*, November 11, 1985; Ian Kershaw, "The Führer Myth: How Hitler Won Over the German People," *Spiegel Online International*, January 30, 2008, accessed November 2015, http://www.spiegel.de/international/germany/the-fuehrer-myth-how-hitler-won-over-the-german-people-a-531909.html.

8   Kershaw, *"Hitler Myth,"* xi.

9   Kershaw, *"Hitler Myth,"* 289–290.

10 Geyer, *"Der Hitler-Mythos,"* 811

MODULE 10
THE EVOLVING DEBATE

KEY POINTS

- The ideas in *The "Hitler Myth"* swiftly became part of the canon of German historical scholarship, and have been used and developed extensively by authors writing more general histories of the Third Reich.*

- The concept of the "Hitler* myth" has been used to illuminate many other forms of dictatorship,* including the extreme right-wing nationalist political ideology of fascism* in Italy, and Stalinism*—the form of communism operating in Soviet Russia* under the leadership of Joseph Stalin.*

- The idea of the "Hitler myth" has informed historical interpretation conducted by public intellectuals, scholars of literature, and academic historians.

Uses and Problems

Although some critics had disagreed with a few of Ian Kershaw's contentions in *The "Hitler Myth": Image and Reality in the Third Reich*, the book's main arguments swiftly came to form part of the consensus— as did the idea of the "Hitler myth" as a separate concept. Right from the outset, any scholar of the Third Reich who dared to discuss the phenomenon without properly acknowledging his or her debt to Kershaw could expect short shrift from reviewers. Thus, when the German historian Detlev Peukert★ failed to cite Kershaw in the relevant chapter of his study *Inside Nazi Germany: Conformity, Opposition and Racism in Everyday Life* (1987), he was sternly taken to task for his cavalier treatment of his sources.[1]

More recently, authors of wide-ranging popular histories of the Third Reich, such as David Welch,* Richard J. Evans,* and Michael

> ❝ Kershaw's study of 'the Hitler myth' was by implication an invitation to compare, not only to find common personal traits [between Hitler and Stalin]—there were more than a few—but to explore the whole politics of mythmaking in both countries, the eventual differences, as well as the scholarly debates on such themes. ❞
>
> Moshe Lewin, "Stalin in the Mirror of the Other"

Burleigh,* have cited Kershaw's book extensively, while placing its ideas within a broader social and political framework.[2] Burleigh, in particular, described *The "Hitler Myth"* as "remarkable" and "the best analysis of the social context of the Führer* cult," while also developing some of its key ideas further than Kershaw himself had done. For instance, Burleigh argued that, while "the broader populace may have created the Hitler myth …, Hitler himself managed the supreme feat of mythologizing the myth-makers themselves in a cycle of mutual adoration. They invested in him, and he invested in them."[3]

Schools of Thought

One of the most important aspects of the reception of *The "Hitler Myth"* has been the ease with which its core concept can be translated into other political contexts. The idea of propagandistic* mythmaking around the figure of a powerful leader can easily be applied to many other totalitarian* regimes or extremist movements ("totalitarian" here signifying a regime in which the state intercedes in the life of the citizen and dissent is suppressed). So, for instance, it has become common to speak of a "Mussolini* myth" in connection with fascist Italy and its leader Benito Mussolini, particularly in studies comparing Italian fascism with National Socialism (Nazism).* Take, for instance, the historian Carl Levy's remark that "the leader principle was essential: the Hitler myth and the Mussolini myth were important in

[both] phases of fascism."[4] More recently, the concept has even been cited in connection with Jörg Haider,* the former leader of the far-right Austrian Freedom Party (FPÖ).*[5]

Scholars have also used the concept of leader mythology in the context of the Soviet Union, this time with reference to the personality cults of Vladimir Lenin* and Joseph Stalin,*[6] two of the nation's leaders. Kershaw himself explored these parallels in collaboration with Russian historian Moshe Lewin* in a collection of essays entitled *Stalinism and Nazism: Dictatorships in Comparison.*[7] In his own contribution to the volume, "Stalin in the Mirror of the Other," Lewin deliberately used Kershaw's model to illuminate Stalin's own dictatorship, remarking that, "not unlike Hitler and his self-identification with the function of Führer, Stalin actually *became the system* and his personality therefore acquired a 'systemic' dimension."[8]

In Current Scholarship

In a sense, all scholars of Nazi Germany are now disciples of Ian Kershaw, and there are few comprehensive studies of the Third Reich today that fail to mention *The "Hitler Myth"*, at least in passing. As the editors of a collection of essays in his honor commented in 2004, "Kershaw's own influence on a wider historiography of twentieth-century Europe" has extended far beyond the students and colleagues who have always worked most closely with him.[9]

However, there are a number of academics who have particularly engaged with the concept of the "Hitler myth" itself. Some are scholars of literature, such as Marcel Atze,* whose work has explored the reception of Hitler's self-mythologization in a number of works of postwar German literature.[10] Others, as one might expect, are historians, such as Erwin Barth, whose detailed study *Joseph Goebbels und die Formierung des Führer-Mythos, 1917 bis 1934* (Joseph Goebbels* and the Formation of the Führer Myth, 1917 to 1934) explores the ways in which Goebbels contributed to the creation of Adolf Hitler's charismatic aura during the Weimar Republic.[11] As one reviewer has noted: "Barth's narrative accords entirely with our current understanding of the Hitler phenomenon, drawing heavily on Ian Kershaw's magisterial work on the subject."[12]

Meanwhile, the British broadcaster and filmmaker Laurence Rees,* in his 2012 book and TV series entitled *The Dark Charisma of Adolf Hitler*, has popularized Kershaw's ideas for a far wider audience.[13] Kershaw himself acted as Rees's historical advisor, and later praised both the book and the series as offering "sharp insight into the adulation of Hitler by millions of Germans that underpinned his 'charismatic rule.'"[14]

NOTES

1   Richard F. Hamilton, "*Inside Nazi Germany: Conformity, Opposition and Racism in Everyday Life* by Detlev J. K. Peukert," *Contemporary Sociology* 17, no. 2 (1988): 189–91. See Detlev J. K. Peukert, *Inside Nazi Germany: Conformity, Opposition and Racism in Everyday Life* (London: Batsford, 1987).

2   See, for instance, David Welch, *The Third Reich: Politics and Propaganda* (London: Routledge, 2002); Richard J. Evans, *The Third Reich in Power* (London: Penguin, 2005); Michael Burleigh, *The Third Reich: A New History* (London: Pan Macmillan, 2000).

3   Burleigh, *The Third Reich*, 846, 267, 931.

4   Carl Levy, "Fascism, National Socialism and Conservatives in Europe, 1914–1945: Issues for Comparativists," *Contemporary European History* 8, no. 1 (1999): 97–126. On the "Mussolini myth," see also Emilio Gentile, *The Struggle for Modernity: Nationalism, Futurism and Fascism* (London: Praeger, 2003).

5   Allyson Fiddler, "Staging Jörg Haider: Protest and Resignation in Elfriede Jelinek's 'Das Lebewohl' and Other Recent Texts for the Theatre," *Modern Language Review* 97, no. 2 (2002): 362.

6   See also Vladimir Tismaneanu, *The Devil in History: Communism, Fascism, and Some Lessons of the Twentieth Century* (Berkeley: University of California Press, 2012); Benno Ennker, "Die Anfänge des Leninkultes," *Jahrbücher für Geschichte Osteuropas* 35, no. 4 (1987): 534–55.

7   Ian Kershaw and Moshe Lewin, eds., *Stalinism and Nazism: Dictatorships in Comparison* (Cambridge: Cambridge University Press, 1997).

8   Moshe Lewin, "Stalin in the Mirror of the Other," in *Stalinism and Nazism: Dictatorships in Comparison*, eds. Ian Kershaw and Moshe Lewin (Cambridge: Cambridge University Press, 1997), 120.

9   Anthony McElligott and Tim Kirk, eds., *Working Towards the Führer: Essays in Honour of Sir Ian Kershaw* (Manchester: Manchester University Press, 2004), 11.

10   Marcel Atze, *"Unser Hitler": Der Hitler-Mythos im Spiegel der deutschsprachigen Literatur nach 1945* (Gottingen: Wallstein, 2003).

11   Erwin Barth, *Joseph Goebbels und die Formierung des Führer-Mythos, 1917 bis 1934* (Erlangen: Palm & Enke, 1999).

12   Conan Fischer, "*Joseph Goebbels und die Formierung des Führer-Mythos, 1917 bis 1934* by Erwin Barth," *English Historical Review* 116, no. 465 (2001): 272.

13   Laurence Rees, *The Dark Charisma of Adolf Hitler: Leading Millions into the Abyss* (London: Ebury Press, 2013).

14   See BBC Media Centre, "The Dark Charisma of Adolf Hitler", accessed February 2, 2016, http://www.bbc.co.uk/mediacentre/proginfo/2012/46/the-dark-charisma-of-adolf-hitler-1.html; https://www.penguin.co.uk/books/1070951/the-dark-charisma-of-adolf-hitler/

IMPACT AND INFLUENCE TODAY

KEY POINTS

- *The "Hitler Myth"* is now regarded as a classic work of German history.

- Recent scholarship on the Nazi* racial community *(Volksgemeinschaft),* and on the degree to which Nazism was met with consent or coercion, has engaged substantially with Kershaw's thesis.

- Scholars continue to debate the applicability of the sociologist* Max Weber's* concept of "charismatic leadership"* to Adolf Hitler*—an idea that Kershaw first popularized in *The "Hitler Myth"*.

Position

Ian Kershaw's *The "Hitler Myth": Image and Reality in the Third Reich* continues to have a wide-ranging impact, more than 25 years after it was first published in Germany. School textbooks, general histories of the German nation, and in-depth studies of the Nazi regime all draw on Kershaw's ideas and concepts.[1] The work has been used to illuminate connections with other totalitarian* regimes, to explore the nature of political leadership, and to provide a springboard for new ideas about life and politics in the Third Reich.*

More recently, scholars have come to see the "Hitler myth" as complementing other forms of Nazi propaganda that encouraged ordinary Germans to consent to the demands made by the National Socialist (Nazi) regime. Foremost among these was the idea of the exclusive racial community (*Volksgemeinschaft*), with its seductive promises of national solidarity and personal fulfillment.[2] As American historians Christopher R. Browning and Lewis H. Siegelbaum have

> ❝ A constant theme of my writing on Hitler and National Socialism has been to suggest that they are best grasped through Max Weber's quasi-religious concept of 'charismatic authority', in which irrational hopes and expectations of salvation are projected onto an individual, who is thereby invested with heroic qualities...
> Of course, manifestations of 'charismatic leadership' were far from confined to Germany in the interwar period. But Hitler's was both different in character and more far-reaching in impact than the charismatic forms seen anywhere else. ❞
> Ian Kershaw, "Hitler and the Uniqueness of Nazism"

argued: "Charismatic identification of Germans with Hitler as the personification of a German renewal transcending the mundane and petty problems and shortcomings of everyday life reinforced the belief in a *Volksgemeinschaft* transcending the divisions of German society. Just as a 'readiness for consensus' underlay Germans' belief that the Third Reich had restored the *Volksgemeinschaft*, Hitler's charisma likewise reflected society's transcendental longings and hopes."[3]

Interaction

Scholars who have focused on the Nazi regime's politics of social consensus, foremost among them Robert Gellately,* have tended to draw substantially on Ian Kershaw's work. Even in the early 1990s, Gellately stressed the need for scholarship on Nazi Germany to avoid the usual stark oppositions between history from "above" and history from "below"—that is, between histories focusing on the actions of those of great political and social status and those dealing with the experience of common people. He concluded that Kershaw was "already working this terrain" with *The "Hitler Myth"*, since it investigated "both the Führer's* image-building *and* image-reception."[4] In his subsequent book-length study *Backing Hitler: Consent and Coercion in Nazi Germany* (2001), Gellately explicitly acknowledged Kershaw's influence in his introduction, stating that "I share some of the views expressed by Ian Kershaw ... [suggesting] that Hitler's own popularity provided one of the main foundations on which the regime was founded and built."[5]

In a sense, Gellately's own survey of the negative inducements to accept Nazi rule—concentration camps,* secret police, informers—can be seen as providing a dark mirror image of the positive motivation fostered by the "Hitler myth." For scholars who wish to understand the German people's attitude to the Holocaust,* Kershaw's work has also provided an important starting point. To take one example, in his study of popular violence against Jews* in provincial Germany between 1919 and 1939, the German historian Michael Wildt* has both mined *The "Hitler Myth"* for material useful for his thesis and engaged with many of Kershaw's other works.[6]

The Continuing Debate
One of the areas where concepts developed in *The "Hitler Myth"* continue to stimulate vigorous debate is the subfield focusing on the nature of totalitarian leadership and political religion. As one scholar has recently noted, "Max Weber used the example of Joseph Smith Jr.,* the founder of the American religion Mormonism,* as the epitome of his notion of charismatic authority in his *Economy and Society*, but Hitler is often considered a better example of such a figure by many scholars today."[7]

Historians and sociologists working on such topics therefore regularly cite Kershaw's work. For instance, in an article published in 2006, one scholar argued that a conceptual line should be drawn between "the charismatization of the Italian and German dictators* by their own particular 'charismatic community,'" as depicted by

Kershaw, and the top-down imposition of a "leadership cult" which is not necessarily based on popular support.[8]

Meanwhile, the French political scientist Michel Dobry* has undertaken an in-depth analysis of Kershaw's use of Max Weber's model of "charismatic leadership," which Kershaw first outlined in the introduction and conclusion to the English edition of *The "Hitler Myth"*. Although Dobry states that Kershaw was far from the first "to have made the link between the historical trajectory of Nazism and Weber's conceptualization of the 'charismatic leader' … the majority of authors only [made] this comparison superficially, without exploring its implications and without fully understanding Weber's idea … this is not the case with Kershaw."[9] Rather, Dobry argues that Kershaw's development of Weber's charismatic model, particularly in his later biographical work on Hitler, "provides a fascinating coherence to the trajectory of the 'Nazi phenomenon.'"[10] Still, it does also contain some idiosyncrasies that are never fully explained, and Dobry criticizes these in detail. For instance, he argues that the charismatic model is unable to explain sufficiently the huge variations in the Nazi Party's electoral performance between 1928 and 1932.[11]

NOTES

1   See, for example, Mary Fulbrook and David Williamson, *OCR History A: Democracy and Dictatorship in Germany 1919–1963* (London: Heinemann, 2008); Mary Fulbrook, *A History of Germany 1918–2014: The Divided Nation* (Oxford: Wiley Blackwell, 2015); Armin Nolzen, "Charismatic Legitimation and Bureaucratic Rule: The NSDAP in the Third Reich, 1933–1945," *German History* 23, no. 4 (2005): 494–518, esp. pp. 515–16.

2   Two useful collections of essays on this theme are provided by Michael Wildt and Frank Bajohr, eds., *Volksgemeinschaft: Neue Forschungen zur Gesellschaft des Nationalsozialismus* (Frankfurt am Main: Fischer, 2009), and Marina Steber and Bernhard Gotto, eds., *Visions of Community in Nazi Germany: Social Engineering and Private Lives* (Oxford: Oxford University Press, 2014); the latter includes a contribution by Kershaw.

3   Christopher R. Browning and Lewis H. Siegelbaum, "Frameworks for

Social Engineering: Stalinist Schema of Identification and the Nazi Volksgemeinschaft," in *Beyond Totalitarianism: Stalinism and Nazism Compared*, eds. Michael Geyer and Sheila Fitzpatrick (Cambridge: Cambridge University Press, 2009), 248.

4   Robert Gellately, "Rethinking the Nazi Terror System: A Historiographical Analysis," *German Studies Review* 14, no. 1 (1991): 26–7.

5   Robert Gellately, *Backing Hitler: Consent and Coercion in Nazi Germany* (Oxford: Oxford University Press, 2001), 3.

6   Michael Wildt, *Hitler's Volksgemeinschaft and the Dynamics of Racial Exclusion: Violence against Jews in Provincial Germany, 1919–1939* (Oxford: Berghahn, 2012), examples on pp. 83, 115–116.

7   Bernard Mees, "Charisma, Authority and *Heil*: Walter Baetke and the Chasm of 1945," in *Nordic Ideology between Religion and Scholarship*, eds. Horst Junginger and Andreas Åkerlund (New York: Peter Lang, 2013), 87–106.

8   Aristotle A. Kallis, "Fascism, 'Charisma' and 'Charismatisation': Weber's Model of 'Charismatic Domination' and Interwar European Fascism," *Totalitarian Movements and Political Religions* 7, no. 1 (2006): 25–43, quotation from p. 32.

9   Michel Dobry, "Hitler, Charisma and Structure: Reflections on Historical Methodology," in *Charisma and Fascism in Interwar Europe*, eds. António Costa Pinto, Roger Eatwell, and Stein Igelvik Larsen (New York: Routledge, 2007), 20.

10 Dobry, "Hitler, Charisma and Structure," 21.

11 Dobry, "Hitler, Charisma and Structure," 23–9. For an analysis that uses the model of charismatic leadership to analyze Hitler's rule, but which does not actively engage with Kershaw's arguments on this theme, see M. Rainer Lepsius, "The Model of Charismatic Leadership and its Applicability to the Rule of Adolf Hitler," *Totalitarian Movements and Political Religions* 7, no. 2 (2006): 175–90, which is also reprinted in the same volume as Dobry's essay (37–52). For a more critical viewpoint, see Ludolf Herbst, *Hitlers Charisma: Die Erfindung eines deutschen Messias* (Frankfurt am Main: Fischer, 2010), although Herbst only covers the period from 1919 to 1934.

WHERE NEXT?

KEY POINTS

- Despite having first appeared in the 1980s, *The "Hitler Myth"* looks set to retain its influence and impact well into the new millennium.

- A new generation of scholars of Adolf Hitler* and the Third Reich,* among them the Cambridge historian and Hitler biographer Brendan Simms,* are still heavily invested in Ian Kershaw's work and theories.

- Ultimately, the insights provided by *The "Hitler Myth"* can help us better understand the global tragedy of World War II* and the Holocaust.*

Potential

Ian Kershaw's *The "Hitler Myth": Image and Reality in the Third Reich* seems set to exert continuing influence on studies of the Third Reich and beyond. Its relevance appears undiminished since its initial publication, even though the field has undoubtedly grown and moved on substantially since the 1980s.

Although *The "Hitler Myth"* is very much a classic text in its own right, it will also be remembered for the foundations that it laid for Ian Kershaw's subsequent work on Adolf Hitler. Just to take one example, the concept of "working towards the Führer,"* which Kershaw used extensively in his two-volume Hitler biography—and which has, like the "Hitler myth", become a familiar term used in studies on the Third Reich—was strongly influenced by the ideas concerning Hitler's charismatic leadership* that Kershaw developed when revising *The "Hitler Myth"* for publication in English.[1] Moreover, the book's enduring relevance is also strongly implied by the number of times it

> 66 Hitler is all researched out. In order to provide enough paper to wrap up all the studies and biographies about him, one would have to uproot every tree in Germany. And yet, time and again, authors come along who sharpen our insights into this era and its ideologies—from Joachim Fest* to Ernst Nolte,* Daniel Jonah Goldhagen*... to Ian Kershaw. Some cause controversy, others disapproval. But they rarely leave people cold. For the hypothesis still holds true, at least implicitly, that whoever can explain Hitler is contributing to an understanding of the Germans. 99
>
> Malte Lehming, "Über links, rechts, Klassen und Rassen hinweg. Antiamerikanismus und Antisemitismus," *Der Tagesspiegel*

has been translated and reissued over the past three decades, even when this has involved no substantial overhauling of the text to incorporate new scholarship.[2]

Finally, the concept of the "Hitler myth" is likely to continue to be useful to scholars working on other dictatorships,* including those that exist in the present day. Although Kershaw warns against trying to construct direct parallels between Hitler and dictators such as the former Serbian president Slobodan Milošević* and the former Iraqi leader Saddam Hussein,* he has noted in at least one interview that "elsewhere in the world, we still have to deal with powerful dictators who might have a strong regional impact."[3]

Future Directions

It remains to be seen whether other scholars of Hitler will take up the gauntlet thrown down by Ian Kershaw in *The "Hitler Myth"*, developing and refining his ideas still further. One possible protagonist in future debates on the nature of Hitler's power could easily be

Brendan Simms, currently professor of the history of European international relations at the University of Cambridge. Simms is in the middle of writing what he terms a "geostrategic" biography of Hitler, tentatively entitled *Hitler: Only the World was Enough.*[4] The book's thesis has already aroused media comment and controversy, particularly in Germany, even before its publication.[5] Simms has long immersed himself in Kershaw's work on Hitler, praising him in the *Times Higher Education* as "the world expert on Adolf Hitler's role in the Third Reich," and singling out for comment the fact that "his earlier studies firmly established the concept of the 'Hitler myth,' the charismatic mechanism by which the dictator won and maintained his extraordinary power over the imagination and lives of the German people."[6] We might therefore expect Simms's new work on the Führer's aims and motivations to draw upon Kershaw's ideas, and upon his body of work more broadly.

Summary

Ian Kershaw's *The "Hitler Myth"* is essential reading for anyone interested in the Third Reich, for anyone with an interest in German or European history more generally, but also for anyone who wants to study the dynamics of power, propaganda, and political leadership. Sociology,* politics, and international relations are all disciplines that can benefit from the broader insights afforded by Kershaw's in-depth study.

One of the book's most enduring legacies is Kershaw's use of the concept of "myth" to describe the personality cult of an authoritarian leader. This idea can easily be transposed to fit other historical times and political situations. Indeed, the notion can prove extremely useful for analyzing leaders of dictatorships, or leaders of extremist movements, much closer to our own time.

Finally, the book helps to explain how one of the greatest disasters in human history—the indescribable slaughter unleashed by World

War II and the Holocaust—could have come to pass. Hitler's dictatorship brought about a tragedy that encompassed the whole world, and that still shapes politics and current affairs today. By contributing to our understanding of Hitler's hold over the German people, *The "Hitler Myth"* helps us come closer to comprehending both the origins of that tragedy, and its global repercussions.

NOTES

1   See Ian Kershaw, "'Working Towards the Führer': Reflections on the Nature of the Hitler Dictatorship," in *Stalinism and Nazism: Dictatorships in Comparison*, eds. Ian Kershaw and Moshe Lewin (Cambridge: Cambridge University Press, 1997), 88–106.

2   Ian Kershaw, *The "Hitler Myth": Image and Reality in the Third Reich* (Oxford: Oxford University Press, 2001), ix.

3   Thomas Roman, "Interview with Ian Kershaw," *Eurozine*, October 24, 2002, accessed October 2015, http://www.eurozine.com/articles/2002-10-24-roman-en.html.

4   Brendan Simms, *Hitler: Only the World was Enough* (London: Penguin, forthcoming). Some of the book's arguments about Hitler's early life are explored in an article that Simms published in *International Affairs* in 2014; see Brendan Simms, "Against a 'World of Enemies': The Impact of the First World War on the Development of Hitler's Ideology," *International Affairs* 90, no. 2 (2014): 317–36.

5   See, for example, Malte Lehming, "Über links, rechts, Klassen und Rassen hinweg. Antiamerikanismus und Antisemitismus," *Der Tagesspiegel*, April 14, 2014.

6   Brendan Simms, "A Last Word on the Führer and the Third Reich: Hitler, 1936–1945," *Times Higher Education*, January 5, 2001.

GLOSSARY

GLOSSARY OF TERMS

Allies: the coalition of countries, led by Great Britain, the Soviet Union, and the United States, that joined together in World War II to fight against the "Axis powers" of Germany, Italy, and Japan.

Alltagsgeschichte: the "history of everyday life" was a form of social history developed by German historians in the 1970s and 1980s, focusing on ordinary people's experiences.

Annexation of the Rhineland: On March 7, 1936, Hitler marched German military forces into the Rhineland area on Germany's western border, an area that the Treaty of Versailles had decreed to be a demilitarized zone.

Anschluss: the term for Hitler's incorporation of Austria into the Third Reich in March 1938.

Anthropology: the study of humankind, commonly conducted through the study of human culture, belief, and society.

Auschwitz: a concentration camp forming a key component in a system of labor and extermination camps run by the Nazi regime in occupied Poland. Over a million prisoners, most of them Jewish, died in the gas chambers of Auschwitz-Birkenau.

Austrian Freedom Party (FPÖ): an Austrian right-wing party, founded in 1956. Jörg Haider led the party in a more populist direction when he became its leader in 1986.

Bavaria: a state in the south of Germany that used to be a separate kingdom until Germany was unified in 1871. At the end of World

War II, Bavaria was occupied by US troops.

Bielefeld School: a group of German historians, led by Hans-Ulrich Wehler, who focused primarily on social history. They presented history as a "social science," rather than focusing on traditional forms of national political history.

Bolshevism: a term for Russian communism, named after the majority faction—the Bolsheviks—of what later became the Communist Party of the Soviet Union.

Bolton Priory: a twelfth-century Augustinian monastery in North Yorkshire, England.

Charismatic leadership: a theory developed by the pioneering sociologist Max Weber, describing a form of power inspired by a leader's exceptional personal qualities.

Communism: a revolutionary ideology that advocates class war and common ownership of property. In communist dictatorships, the state tends to control all aspects of society.

Concentration camp: a punitive camp where large numbers of people are interned, especially political prisoners or persecuted minorities. Inmates are often made to perform forced labor, or they may be imprisoned until their execution.

Cultural studies: a politically oriented field of inquiry drawing on the aims and methods of many different academic fields, commonly sociology, political science, history, philosophy, and literary theory.

Dictator: a leader whose authority over the state and its citizens is absolute.

Fascism: a form of right-wing, nationalistic, and authoritarian government. Mussolini originally used the term when he founded his National Fascist Party in Italy in 1921.

Federal Republic of Germany (West Germany): the half of Germany that had been occupied by the Allies at the end of World War II, and which became a democratic republic run from Bonn until reunification with the German Democratic Republic in 1990.

Final Solution: the Nazi regime's policy of systematic extermination of all European Jews, which resulted in the Holocaust.

Führer: the German word for leader; a title now most associated with Adolf Hitler.

Functionalism: a school of thought that argues that Hitler's power over Nazi Germany was limited by the competing, chaotic power structures of the regime, and that the Holocaust developed through a combination of radicalizing factors, rather than being dictated by Hitler's will alone.

Genocide: the mass killing of a group of people, particularly on ethnic grounds.

German Democratic Republic (East Germany): a Soviet-controlled dictatorship established in the half of Germany that was occupied by the Russians at the end of World War II.

Goethe Institute: a worldwide network of nonprofit institutions that promote the German language and foster international cultural cooperation. The institutes offer language courses, as well as more general information on German politics, culture, and society.

Holocaust: the mass murder of approximately six million Jews by the Nazi regime between 1941 and 1945.

Imperialist: someone engaged in empire building.

Institut für Zeitgeschichte: the Institute for Contemporary History in Munich was founded by the Allies in the late 1940s in order to stimulate research into the Nazi past. Researchers at the Institute were dedicated to promoting new forms of social history, such as *Alltagsgeschichte* (the history of everyday life), as well as helping to bring Nazi crimes to justice.

Intentionalism: a school of thought that argues that Nazi Germany was primarily ruled according to Hitler's will and ideology, and that he was directly responsible for the Holocaust.

Iron Curtain: the notional boundary separating Communist Eastern Europe from Western Europe in the period between 1945 and 1991.

"Jewish question": the debate on how Jewish minorities should be treated in European society. Hitler's answer to the question was ultimately provided by the "Final Solution"—mass genocide.

Jews: An ethno-religious group related to the ancient Hebrews. Throughout the centuries they have often been subjected to extreme prejudice.

Micro-history: a form of history that challenges the generalizations that are often made in traditional forms of social history, focusing instead on a single event, individual, or community.

Mormonism: a term defining the religious beliefs and practices of the Church of Jesus Christ of the Latter-Day Saints, which are significantly different from those of traditional Christian Churches, such as Protestantism and Catholicism.

Munich Agreement: an international settlement, made in 1938, that allowed Hitler to annex the Sudetenland—those borderlands of Czechoslovakia inhabited by a majority of German speakers.

Nazism/National Socialism: the far-right ideology put forward by Hitler and the National Socialist German Workers' Party (NSDAP). Key traits include racism, anti-Semitism, and German nationalism.

Night of the Long Knives: the purge of Ernst Röhm and the SA (*Sturmabteilung*) that took place from June 30 to July 2, 1934, at Hitler's instigation.

1968 Student Revolutions: a wave of left-wing protest and unrest among university students that, though it was most violent in France, spread throughout Europe and the United States.

Polycracy: government by many rulers—a term commonly used for the competing power structures within the Third Reich.

Propaganda: messages and information disseminated through broadcast, print, and digital media with the express aim of influencing an audience to adopt a particular, generally political, perspective or set of opinions; propaganda is considered an important component in the establishment of a cult of personality such as that enjoyed by Adolf Hitler.

Psychoanalysis: a therapeutic and theoretical approach to understanding the workings of the unconscious mind, established by the Austrian neurologist Sigmund Freud in the late nineteenth century.

Psychohistory: an approach that attempts to fuse insights from psychotherapy with historical methodology, in order to explain the possible psychological motivations of historical figures.

Roman Catholic: the Roman Catholic Church is the largest and oldest of the Christian denominations. The head of the Catholic Church is the Pope, who resides in the Vatican in Italy. Approximately half of all Christians worldwide are Catholics.

Royal Air Force (RAF): the aerial combat wing of the British armed forces, founded in 1918.

SA (Sturmabteilung): the Nazi Party paramilitary wing, heavily involved in street violence against other parties in the movement's early years. After its leaders were assassinated in 1934, the SA quickly lost power and influence.

Semiotics: the study of the construction and communication of meaning through signs and symbols, notably in language.

Social history: an area of history that first became popular in the 1960s and 1970s. It focuses on the experiences of ordinary people rather than the actions of "great men."

Socialism: a political movement aiming to establish common ownership of the means of production, and to equalize society.

Sociology: the study of human behavior, social structures, and institutions.

Soviet Union (USSR): the Union of Soviet Socialist Republics was a communist state that encompassed Russia and its surrounding states in Eastern Europe and Central Asia. The Soviet regime lasted from 1922 until 1991.

SS (Schutzstaffel): originally Hitler's bodyguard, the SS became the corps responsible for the police and terror apparatus within the Nazi state. Members of the SS were supposed to represent a political and racial elite.

Stalinism: the form of communism advocated by Joseph Stalin during his dictatorship over the Soviet Union, characterized in particular by state terror, suppression of dissidents, and a totalitarian state apparatus.

Strukturgeschichte: the German term for structural history, a form of "total history" propounded by the Bielefeld School that used a social scientific approach, focusing on societal processes rather than the actions of elites.

Sudetenland: a region of northern Bohemia and Moravia with a predominantly German-speaking population, which became part of Czechoslovakia after World War I. In 1938, Hitler demanded that, due to its German majority, the Sudetenland should be ceded to Germany, or he would annex the region by force. This resulted in the Munich Agreement.

Term of art: a term with a sense appropriate to a specific context.

Third Reich: a term for Germany between 1933 and 1945, when it was ruled by Hitler and the National Socialist (Nazi) regime.

Totalitarian: a regime in which the state intrusively intervenes in the life of the citizen and dissent is suppressed.

Totalitarianism theory: a theory that argues for equivalence between fascist and communist dictatorships, focusing on similarities in ideology, the presence of a one-party state, a state terror apparatus, a state monopoly on violence and mass communication, and centralized decision-making.

Transnationalism: an approach to history that tries to make connections between different countries, rather than focusing on individual nation-states. It first gained popularity in the 2000s.

Treaty of Versailles: one of the peace treaties that concluded World War I, it placed heavy sanctions on Germany, including reducing the German armed forces to a negligible quota, allowing French troops to occupy the Rhineland, and seizing German territory in central Europe. It was widely hated and despised by Germans, who considered it an insult to their country's sovereignty.

Vierteljahrshefte für Zeitgeschichte (Contemporary History Quarterly): the Institut für Zeitgeschichte's in-house journal, in which much of its groundbreaking research was first published.

Volksgemeinschaft: German term for the national community, often defined by race. In Nazi Germany, Jews, Gypsies, homosexuals, the mentally deficient, and other groups deemed biologically inferior were automatically excluded from the *Volksgemeinschaft*.

Weimar Republic: the name given to Germany between 1919 and 1933, during which time a democratic constitution was established in the aftermath of World War I.

World War I: an international conflict that took place between 1914 and 1918, centered in Europe, and involving the major world powers of the day. At its end, Germany was defeated, but not occupied, by its opponents.

World War II: a global war that involved all of the world's great powers and numerous other countries around the globe. The war resulted in an estimated 50–85 million deaths. Its outbreak was motivated by Hitler's desire to conquer an empire across Europe and Western Russia that would equal the United States.

PEOPLE MENTIONED IN THE TEXT

Marcel Atze (b. 1967) is a scholar of German literature based at the Fritz Bauer Institute, Frankfurt am Main. His best-known work has focused on the reception of the "Hitler myth" in postwar German literature.

Karl Dietrich Bracher (b. 1922) is a German historian and political scientist whose research has focused predominantly on Germany in the first half of the twentieth century, and on totalitarianism. His best-known work is *The German Dictatorship: The Origins, Structure, and Effects of National Socialism* (1969).

John Breuilly (b. 1946) is professor of nationalism and ethnicity at the London School of Economics. He has published numerous works on the theory of nationalism.

Christopher Brooke (1927–2015) is emeritus professor of ecclesiastical history at the University of Cambridge, and a fellow of Gonville and Caius College. He has published extensively on medieval Church history.

Martin Broszat (1926–89) was one of the most prominent historians in postwar Germany, known particularly for his studies of the Third Reich and of Nazi crimes against the Jews. He directed the *Institut für Zeitgeschichte* in Munich for 17 years.

Michael Burleigh (b. 1955) is one of Britain's most prominent public historians. Much of his work has focused on the Third Reich, including *The Racial State: Germany 1933–1945* and *The Third Reich: A New History*.

William Carr (1921–91) was a British historian of modern Germany and a professor at the University of Sheffield. He is best known for his classic textbook *A History of Germany: 1815–1990.*

Michel Dobry is a French sociologist and political scientist, noted for his work on political crises and fascism. Since September 2001, he has taught at the Pantheon-Sorbonne, a college of the University of Paris.

Richard J. Evans (b. 1947) is the former Regius Professor of History at the University of Cambridge, and the president of Wolfson College. His most famous work is his best-selling *Third Reich Trilogy*, published by Penguin. In 2012 he was knighted for services to scholarship.

Joachim Fest (1926–2006) was a prominent German journalist and scholar, best known for his biography of Hitler, which appeared in 1973. For many years, he edited the culture section of the *Frankfurter Allgemeine Zeitung*, Germany's leading newspaper.

Robert Gellately (b. 1943) is a Canadian historian and a professor of history at Florida State University. He made his name with his research on the Gestapo and the Nazi terror system.

Michael Geyer (b. 1947) is an emeritus professor of modern German and European history at the University of Chicago. He is particularly known for his work on war, violence, and death in twentieth-century Germany.

Joseph Goebbels (1897–1945) was the Reich minister of propaganda in Nazi Germany, and a devoted follower of Hitler since the mid-1920s.

Daniel Jonah Goldhagen (b. 1959) is an American author, formerly based at Harvard University. He gained worldwide renown with his highly controversial book *Hitler's Willing Executioners: Ordinary Germans and the Holocaust* (1996), which argued that Germans had always had an inborn tendency to hate Jews.

Jörg Haider (1950–2008) was the leader of the right-wing Austrian Freedom Party (FPÖ) for many years. He was also the governor of Carinthia, a province of Austria, for more than a decade.

Klaus Hildebrand (b. 1941) is a German historian and an emeritus professor at the University of Bonn. He specializes in military and political history.

Andreas Hillgruber (1925–89) was a controversial German historian of the Third Reich. He was heavily involved in the Historians' Dispute (*Historikerstreit*) of the late 1980s, arguing against the uniqueness of the Holocaust in his book *Zweierlei Untergang: Die Zerschlagung des Deutschen Reiches und das Ende des europäischen Judentums* (Two Kinds of Ruin: The Fall of the German Reich and the End of European Jewry), which was published in 1986.

Adolf Hitler (1889–1945) was the leader of the National Socialist (Nazi) Party, and chancellor of Germany between 1933 and 1945. He ruled the Third Reich as a fascist dictatorship, and was responsible for millions of deaths caused by World War II and the Holocaust, which he instigated.

Saddam Hussein (1937–2006) was a dictator who ruled Iraq as its fifth president between 1979 and 2003. He was executed in 2006, following his capture during the American invasion of Iraq in 2003.

Eberhard Jäckel (b. 1929) is a German historian and emeritus professor at the University of Stuttgart. He is best known for his work on Hitler and the Third Reich, particularly *Hitlers Weltanschauung* (1969).

Jürgen Kocka (b. 1941) is an emeritus professor at the Free University, Berlin. Along with Hans-Ulrich Wehler, he was one of the key figures in the Bielefeld School of social history.

Vladimir Lenin (1870–1924) was one of the key architects of the Soviet State, and the leader of the Russian Communist Party. He led the Bolshevik Revolution in 1917, which deposed democracy in Russia.

Moshe Lewin (1921–2010) was a leading historian of Soviet Russia. Until his retirement in 1995, he was a professor at the University of Pennsylvania.

Timothy Mason (1940–90) was a specialist in the social history of the Third Reich. His left-wing views led him to concentrate on the history of the working class. His most important essays are collected in *Nazism, Fascism and the Working Class* (1995).

Slobodan Milošević (1941–2006) was the former president of Serbia (1989–1997) and of the Federal Republic of Yugoslavia (1997–2000). He was charged with having committed crimes against humanity and genocide in Bosnia, Croatia, and Kosovo during the Balkan wars of the 1990s.

Alan Milward (1935–2010) was a European economic historian. He was particularly interested in the dynamics of European integration. He spent much of his professional life as a professor at Manchester University, and then at the London School of Economics.

Hans Mommsen (1930–2015) was one of Germany's leading historians of the Third Reich. He is most famous for his view that the Holocaust resulted from a process of "cumulative radicalization" of the German state under Nazism, rather than being directly planned by Hitler.

Benito Mussolini (1883–1945) was the creator and leader of the Italian Fascist Party. He ruled Italy as a dictator from 1922 until 1943.

Ernst Nolte (b. 1923) is one of Germany's most notorious historians of the twentieth century. He courted controversy with his revisionist argument that the Holocaust was a response to the threat of Bolshevism, and that Hitler might have had rational reasons for attacking the Jews.

Detlev Peukert (1950–90) was an expert on the social and cultural history of twentieth-century Germany. He was particularly interested in the history of everyday life (*Alltagsgeschichte*), of which he was one of the most influential proponents.

Laurence Rees (b. 1957) is a British broadcaster and writer. He has produced many programs and books dealing with Nazi Germany and the Holocaust, including *The Nazis: A Warning from History* and *The Dark Charisma of Adolf Hitler*.

Ernst Röhm (1887–1934) was one of the first leading members of the Nazi Party and the leader of the SA (*Sturmabteilung*), the Nazi paramilitary wing. Hitler feared him as a potential rival, and ordered his assassination, along with many other prominent SA members, in 1934.

Brendan Simms (b. 1967) is professor of the history of European international relations at the University of Cambridge, and a fellow of Peterhouse. He has published extensively on European history and geopolitics, and is currently writing a "geostrategic" biography of Hitler.

Joseph Smith Jr. (1805–44) was the founder of the religious movement known as Mormonism, or the Church of Jesus Christ of the Latter-Day Saints. Adherents of the movement believe that Smith was a heaven-sent prophet.

Joseph Stalin (1878–1953) was the leader of the Soviet Union's communist dictatorship from the 1920s until his death in 1953. Under his rule, many millions of people died, either at his orders or due to his agricultural policies, which caused widespread famine.

Eric Stone (1924–93) was a medieval historian and a fellow of Keble College, Oxford. Stone was heavily involved in reforming the college and improving its academic standards, but he published very little.

Max Weber (1864–1920) was one of the founders of modern sociology, as well as an influential political philosopher. He is perhaps best known for his book *The Protestant Ethic and the Spirit of Capitalism*, first published in 1905.

Hans-Ulrich Wehler (1931–2014) was one of postwar Germany's most distinguished historians, and the founder of the Bielefeld School of social history. His most important work is still his five-volume *Deutsche Gesellschaftsgeschichte* (History of German Society).

David Welch (b. 1950) is an emeritus professor at the University of Kent. His work specializes in twentieth-century political propaganda, with a particular focus on the Third Reich.

Michael Wildt (b. 1954) is professor of German history at the Humboldt University in Berlin. He is best known for his work on perpetrators of the Holocaust.

Kaiser Wilhelm II (1859–1941) was the last emperor of Germany and king of Prussia. He came to power in 1888 and ruled until 1914, when he abdicated following Germany's defeat in World War I.

WORKS CITED

WORKS CITED

Atze, Marcel. *"Unser Hitler": Der Hitler-Mythos im Spiegel der deutschsprachigen Literatur nach 1945*. Gottingen: Wallstein, 2003.

Baird, Jay W. *"The "Hitler Myth": Image and Reality in the Third Reich* by Ian Kershaw." *American Historical Review* 95, no. 5 (1990): 1569–70.

Barth, Erwin. *Joseph Goebbels und die Formierung des Führer-Mythos, 1917 bis 1934*. Erlangen: Palm & Enke, 1999.

Breuilly, John. "Personal Reflections on Ian Kershaw." In *Working Towards the Führer: Essays in Honour of Sir Ian Kershaw*, edited by Anthony McElligott and Tim Kirk, 260–4. Manchester: Manchester University Press, 2004.

Broszat, Martin. *Der Staat Hitlers: Grundlegung und Entwicklung seiner inneren Verfassung*. Munich: Deutscher Taschenbuch-Verlag, 1969.

- - -*Nach Hitler: Der schwierige Umgang mit unserer Geschichte*. Munich: Oldenbourg, 1987.

- - -"Soziale Motivation und Führer-Bindung des Nationalsozialismus." *Vierteljahrshefte für Zeitgeschichte 49* (1970): 392–409.

Browning, Christopher R., and Lewis H. Siegelbaum. "Frameworks for Social Engineering: Stalinist Schema of Identification and the Nazi Volksgemeinschaft." In *Beyond Totalitarianism: Stalinism and Nazism Compared*, edited by Michael Geyer and Sheila Fitzpatrick, 231–63. Cambridge: Cambridge University Press, 2009.

Burleigh, Michael. *The Third Reich: A New History*. London: Pan Macmillan, 2000.

Crace, John. "Ian Kershaw: Past Master," *Guardian*, June 5, 2007. Accessed October 2015. http://www.theguardian.com/education/2007/jun/05/highereducationprofile.academicexperts.

Crew, David F. "*Alltagsgeschichte*: A New Social History 'From Below'?" *Central European History* 22, nos. 3/4 (1989): 394–407.

Dobry, Michel. "Hitler, Charisma and Structure: Reflections on Historical Methodology." In *Charisma and Fascism in Interwar Europe*, edited by António Costa Pinto, Roger Eatwell, and Stein Igelvik Larsen, 19–36. New York: Routledge, 2007.

Eatwell, Roger. "The Rebirth of Right-Wing Charisma? The Cases of Jean-Marie le Pen and Vladimir Zhirinovsky." *Totalitarian Movements and Political Religions* 3, no. 3 (2002): 1–23.

Ennker, Benno. "Die Anfänge des Leninkultes." *Jahrbücher für Geschichte Osteuropas* 35, no. 4 (1987): 534–55.

Evans, Richard J. *In Hitler's Shadow: West German Historians and the Attempt to Escape from the Nazi Past.* New York: Pantheon, 1989.

- - -*The Third Reich in Power.* London: Penguin, 2005.

Fest, Joachim C. *Hitler: Eine Biographie.* Berlin: Propyläen Verlag, 1973.

Fiddler, Allyson. "Staging Jörg Haider: Protest and Resignation in Elfriede Jelinek's 'Das Lebewohl' and Other Recent Texts for the Theatre." *Modern Language Review* 97, no. 2 (2002): 353–64.

Fischer, Conan. "*Joseph Goebbels und die Formierung des Führer-Mythos, 1917 bis 1934* by Erwin Barth." *English Historical Review* 116, no. 465 (2001): 272–3.

Fox, John P. "*The Ideological Origins of Nazi Imperialism* by Woodruff D. Smith and *The 'Hitler Myth': Image and Reality in the Third Reich* by Ian Kershaw." *International Affairs* 64, no. 2 (1988): 292–3.

Frei, Norbert, ed. *Martin Broszat, der "Staat Hitlers" und die Historisierung des Nationalsozialismus.* Göttingen: Wallstein, 2007.

Fulbrook, Mary. "German Historiography after 1945 Reconsidered." *Bulletin of the German Historical Institute London* 13, no. 1 (1991): 3–9.

- - - *German National Identity after the Holocaust*. Cambridge: Polity Press, 1999.

- - - *A History of Germany 1918–2014: The Divided Nation.* Oxford: Wiley Blackwell, 2015.

Fulbrook, Mary, and David Williamson. *OCR History A: Democracy and Dictatorship in Germany 1919–1963.* London: Heinemann, 2008.

Gellately, Robert. *Backing Hitler: Consent and Coercion in Nazi Germany.* Oxford: Oxford University Press, 2001.

- - - "Rethinking the Nazi Terror System: A Historiographical Analysis." *German Studies Review* 14, no. 1 (1991): 23–38.

Gentile, Emilio. *The Struggle for Modernity: Nationalism, Futurism and Fascism.* London: Praeger, 2003.

Geyer, Michael. "*Der Hitler-Mythos: Volksmeinung und Propaganda im Dritten Reich* by Ian Kershaw." *Journal of Modern History* 54, no. 4 (1982): 811–12.

Geyer, Michael, and Sheila Fitzpatrick, eds. *Beyond Totalitarianism: Stalinism and Nazism Compared.* Cambridge: Cambridge University Press, 2009.

Grill, Johnpeter Horst. "Local and Regional Studies on National Socialism: A Review." *Journal of Contemporary History* 21, no. 2 (1986): 253–94.

Hacke, Jens. "Sammelrez: Ian Kershaw: Der Hitler-Mythos," H-Soz-Kult, November 30, 2000. Accessed November 2015. https://www.h-net.org/reviews/showpdf.php?id=18575.

Hamilton, Richard F. "*Inside Nazi Germany: Conformity, Opposition and Racism in Everyday Life* by Detlev J. K. Peukert." *Contemporary Sociology* 17, no. 2 (1988): 189–91.

Herbst, Ludolf. *Hitlers Charisma: Die Erfindung eines deutschen Messias.* Frankfurt am Main: Fischer, 2010.

Kacandes, Irene. "Klaus L. Berghahn and Jost Hermand, eds., *Unmasking Hitler: Cultural Representations of Hitler from the Weimar Republic to the Present.*" *German Quarterly* 80, no. 4 (2007): 544–5.

Kallis, Aristotle A. "Fascism, 'Charisma' and 'Charismatisation': Weber's Model of 'Charismatic Domination' and Interwar European Fascism." *Totalitarian Movements and Political Religions* 7, no. 1 (2006): 25–43.

Kater, Michael H. "*The 'Hitler Myth': Image and Reality in the Third Reich* by Ian Kershaw." *English Historical Review* 103, no. 409 (1988): 1014–16.

Kershaw, Ian. "Beware the Moral High Ground." *Times Literary Supplement*, October 10, 2003.

- - - *Bolton Priory: The Economy of a Northern Monastery, 1268–1325*. Oxford: Oxford University Press, 1973.

- - - *The End: Hitler's Germany, 1944–45*. London: Penguin, 2011.

- - - *Fateful Choices: Ten Decisions that Changed the World, 1940–1941*. London: Penguin, 2007.

- - - "The Führer Myth: How Hitler Won Over the German People." *Spiegel Online International*, January 30, 2008. Accessed November 2015. http://www.spiegel.de/international/germany/the-fuehrer-myth-how-hitler-won-over-the-german-people-a-531909.html.

- - - *Hitler, 1889–1936: Hubris.* London: Penguin, 1998.

- - - *Hitler, 1936–1946*: *Nemesis.* London: Penguin, 2000.

- - - "Hitler and the Uniqueness of Nazism." *Journal of Contemporary History* 39, no. 2 (2004): 239–54.

- - - *Hitler: A Profile in Power*. London: Longman, 1991.

- - - "The Hitler Myth." *History Today*, November 11, 1985.

- - - *The "Hitler Myth": Image and Reality in the Third Reich,* Oxford: Oxford University Press, 2001.

- - - *Der Hitler-Mythos: Führerkult und Volksmeinung*. Stuttgart: Deutsche Verlags-Anstalt, 1999.

- - - *Der Hitler-Mythos: Volksmeinung und Propaganda im Dritten Reich (Schriftenreihe der Vierteljahrshefte für Zeitgeschichte)*. Stuttgart: Deutsche Verlags-Anstalt, 1980.

- - - *Hitler, the Germans, and the Final Solution.* New Haven: Yale University Press, 2008.

- - - *Making Friends with Hitler: Lord Londonderry and Britain's Road to War*. London: Penguin, 2004.

- - - *The Nazi Dictatorship: Problems and Perspectives of Interpretation.* London: Bloomsbury, 2000.

- - - *Popular Opinion and Political Dissent in the Third Reich: Bavaria 1933–1945.* Oxford: Oxford University Press, 1983.

- - - "Soziale Motivation und Führer-Bindung im Staat Hitlers." In *Martin Broszat, der "Staat Hitlers" und die Historisierung des Nationalsozialismus*, edited by Norbert Frei, 76–84. Göttingen: Wallstein, 2007.

- - - "'Working Towards the Führer': Reflections on the Nature of the Hitler Dictatorship." In *Stalinism and Nazism: Dictatorships in Comparison*, edited by Ian Kershaw and Moshe Lewin, 88–106. Cambridge: Cambridge University Press, 1997.

Kershaw, Ian, and Moshe Lewin, eds. *Stalinism and Nazism: Dictatorships in Comparison.* Cambridge: Cambridge University Press, 1997.

Kitchen, Martin. "*The 'Hitler Myth': Image and Reality in the Third Reich* by Ian Kershaw." *Social History* 14, no. 1 (1989): 141–2.

Lehming, Malte. "Über links, rechts, Klassen und Rassen hinweg. Antiamerikanismus und Antisemitismus." *Der Tagesspiegel*, April 14, 2014.

Lepsius, M. Rainer. "The Model of Charismatic Leadership and its Applicability to the Rule of Adolf Hitler." *Totalitarian Movements and Political Religions* 7, no. 2 (2006): 175–90.

Levy, Carl. "Fascism, National Socialism and Conservatives in Europe, 1914–1945: Issues for Comparativists." *Contemporary European History* 8, no. 1 (1999): 97–126.

Lewin, Moshe. "Stalin in the Mirror of the Other." In *Stalinism and Nazism: Dictatorships in Comparison*, edited by Ian Kershaw and Moshe Lewin, 107–34. Cambridge: Cambridge University Press, 1997.

Lindenfeld, David F. "*The "Hitler Myth": Image and Reality in the Third Reich* by Ian Kershaw." *German Studies Review* 11, no. 2 (1988): 329.

Lorenz, Chris. "Has the Third Reich become History? Martin Broszat as Historian and Pedagogue." *Bulletin of the Arnold and Leona Finkler Institute for Holocaust Research* 8 (1998): 27–44.

Maier, Charles S. *The Unmasterable Past: History, Holocaust, and German National Identity.* Cambridge, MA: Harvard University Press, 1988.

Mason, Timothy W. "Intention and Explanation: A Current Controversy about the Interpretation of National Socialism." In *Der 'Führerstaat': Mythos und Realität. Studien zur Struktur und Politik des Dritten Reiches*, edited by Gerhard Hirschfeld and Lothar Kettenacker, 23–40. Stuttgart: Klett-Cotta, 1981.

- - - "Open Questions on Nazism." In *People's History and Socialist Theory*, edited by Rupert Samuel, 205–10. London: Routledge, 1981.

Matthäus, Jürgen: "*Hitler, the Germans, and the Final Solution* by Ian Kershaw." *Central European History* 42, no. 3 (2009): 582–4.

McElligott, Anthony, and Tim Kirk, eds. *Working Towards the Führer: Essays in Honour of Sir Ian Kershaw.* Manchester: Manchester University Press, 2004.

Mees, Bernard. "Charisma, Authority and *Heil*: Walter Baetke and the Chasm of 1945." In *Nordic Ideology between Religion and Scholarship*, edited by Horst Junginger and Andreas Åkerlund, 87–106. New York: Peter Lang, 2013.

Millum, Danny. Interview with Ian Kershaw, May 14, 2008. Accessed October 2015. http://www.history.ac.uk/makinghistory/resources/interviews/Kershaw_Ian.html.

Mommsen, Hans. *From Weimar to Auschwitz*. Princeton: Princeton University Press, 1991.

Moss, Stephen. "A Life in Writing: Ian Kershaw." *Guardian*, August 17, 2011.

Nicholls, David. *Adolf Hitler: A Biographical Companion.* Oxford: ABC-CLIO, 2000.

Nolzen, Armin. "Charismatic Legitimation and Bureaucratic Rule: The NSDAP in the Third Reich, 1933–1945." *German History* 23, no. 4 (2005): 494–518.

Nyomarkay, Joseph. *Charisma and Factionalism within the Nazi Party.* Minneapolis: University of Minnesota Press, 1967.

Peukert, Detlev J. K. *Inside Nazi Germany: Conformity, Opposition and Racism in Everyday Life.* London: Batsford, 1987.

Rees, Laurence. *The Dark Charisma of Adolf Hitler: Leading Millions into the Abyss.* London: Ebury Press, 2013.

Roman, Thomas. "Interview with Ian Kershaw." *Eurozine*, October 24, 2002. Accessed October 2015. http://www.eurozine.com/articles/2002-10-24-roman-en.html.

Sheffield, University Library. "The Sir Ian Kershaw Collection." Accessed November 2015. http://www.sheffield.ac.uk/library/special/Kershaw.

Simms, Brendan. "Against a 'World of Enemies': The Impact of the First World War on the Development of Hitler's Ideology." *International Affairs* 90, no. 2 (2014): 317–36.

- - - "A Last Word on the Führer and the Third Reich: Hitler, 1936–1945." *Times Higher Education*, January 5, 2001.

Hitler: Only the World was Enough. London: Penguin, forthcoming.

Snyder, Timothy. "In Defense of Bloodlands." *Tablet*, August 3, 2012. Accessed November 2015. http://www.tabletmag.com/jewish-arts-and-culture/ books/108229/in-defense-of-bloodlands.

Steber, Marina, and Bernhard Gotto, eds. *Visions of Community in Nazi Germany: Social Engineering and Private Lives.* Oxford: Oxford University Press, 2014.

Tismaneanu, Vladimir. *The Devil in History: Communism, Fascism, and Some Lessons of the Twentieth Century.* Berkeley: University of California Press, 2012.

Turner, Henry Ashby. "*Hitler, 1936–1946: Nemesis* by Ian Kershaw." *Journal of Modern History* 75, no. 1 (2003): 214–16.

Wasserstein, Bernard. "*Hitler, 1936–1946: Nemesis* by Ian Kershaw." *English Historical Review* 118, no. 475 (2003): 162–4.

Welch, David. *The Third Reich: Politics and Propaganda.* London: Routledge, 2002.

Wildt, Michael. *Hitler's* Volksgemeinschaft *and the Dynamics of Racial Exclusion: Violence against Jews in Provincial Germany, 1919–1939.* Oxford: Berghahn, 2012.

"'Wenn das der Führer wüßte.' Ian Kershaw über Entstehung und Wirkung des Hitler-Mythos." *Die Zeit*, March 30, 2000.

- - - Wildt, Michael, and Frank Bajohr, eds. *Volksgemeinschaft: Neue Forschungen zur Gesellschaft des Nationalsozialismus.* Frankfurt am Main: Fischer, 2009.

Printed in the United States
by Baker & Taylor Publisher Services